The Way to Happiness

D1028484

The Way to Happiness

A Theory of Religion

Don Cupitt

The Way to Happiness

Published in 2005 by Polebridge Press, P.O. Box 6144, Santa Rosa, California 95406.

Library of Congress Cataloging-in-Publication Data

Cupitt, Don.
    The way to happiness : a theory of religion / Don Cupitt.
        p. cm.
    Includes bibliographical references and index.
    ISBN 0-944344-53-4
    1. Religion--Philosophy. I. Title.

BL51.C843 2005
200--dc22

                                                        2004050510

Preface

About 200 years ago, amongst the early Romantics, several people put forward a view of religion as cosmic emotion. They described a kind of feeling that has soared beyond its ordinary biological basis and setting to become universal. Such feeling, by freeing us from anxiety and self-concern, can be profoundly liberating and a great source of happiness.

For English readers, these ideas are especially associated with the young William Wordsworth. It has struck me that by taking them up again and developing them we may be able to show how it is possible to combine a fully naturalistic view of what religion is and how it works with a serious personal practice of religion.

I am a person who holds such views. I actively cultivate a thoroughly religious view of life, of the world, and of all other living beings and regard it as the best way to gain personal religious happiness. I even practise Christianity. But I take an entirely naturalistic view of what religious feeling is and how it works, and I do not personally believe in the objective truth of any Christian dogmas. Developments in philosophy, and historical research into Christian origins, have between them undone traditional doctrinal belief. At most, Christian ideas may be regarded as symbols that have been found to be efficacious in transmuting biologically conditioned emotions into cosmic religious feeling — but that is all of 'truth' that we need.

Thanks to the usual young friends and former students for their comments and criticisms. This time they include Clare Carlisle and Hugh Rayment-Pickard.

Cambridge, 2003
Don Cupitt

Synopsis

Part analytical table of contents and part subject-index, this synopsis is another attempt to make my writing as reader-friendly as possible. It supplies a note of the first occurrence in the text of each of the book's main theses, together with a note of the subsidiary theses, topics discussed, definitions, and so forth, for which the reader may be looking.

Theories of religion: Georges Bataille, *After God* 1; the religious meaning of ordinariness 2, 3; *Not the secularization of religion, but the sacralization of life* 3; empirical study of ordinary language as a method of religious enquiry 4, 5; how the present world and the world to come became one and the same 5, 6; giving up historical religion 6; Jesus slips away 7; *Only the present exists* 8;

First sketch 8; profanities 8, 9; *religious utterances discharge cosmic feelings* 9; they are essentially non-realistic 9; in which respect religious feeling is unlike sexual feeling 10, 11; how we differ from animals 11; Lancelot Andrewes 12; *It All* 12; *eternal happiness* defined 13; the religious object 13; the worlds of childhood and of ordinariness compared 14; ordinary language's treatment of the religious object: *things, everything, it, It All, life* 15; *fate* and *luck* 16; ordinary language is unspeculative 17; its treatment of belief 18; what one lives by 19; commitment to life 20, 21; the traditional functions of religious language 22; the modern functions: *saying yes to time, contingency, and finitude* 22, 23; Nietzsche 23; what can help us to become solar? 24-27; the coolness of sacred love 27, 28; in defence of cool or 'white' love 28; joy in affliction 30; seven maxims for post-dogmatic religion: *there is no specially privileged right vocabulary*, etc. 30; the religion of immediate ethical commitment just to this life, now 31; *ordinary language is the beginning of the world* 32, 33; the meaning of death 33–35.; owning one's own life 35;

Second sketch: *thinking in riffs* 36; *religion is cosmic emotion* 37; our need to publicize and share our feelings 37; *language can actually elicit the feeling that it clothes* 37, 38; thus Culture in a certain sense precedes Nature 38, 39; *language makes you think* 40; *religious love and gratitude are non-objective* 40-41; a Lake District anecdote 41; world love 42; Feuerbach 42; Leibniz and the Problem of Evil 42; *religious expressions resolve conflicting feelings* 43f.; for example, about death 44ff.; everything is immanent, everything happens within language 47; how unreconstructed men can with advantage learn a few things from women 48, 49; true religion is to be in love with ordinary life 51; but we cannot promise total security and exemption from affliction 59. The history of feeling, since Shaftesbury (1699) 54; emotional intelligence 56; the traditional supernaturalism of reason 57; *objective reason, a public and social creation* 58; in defence of clichés 58; democratic philosophy 59., John Virgo 59; transient beauties 60-61; 'Look thy last on all things lovely' 61; solar spirituality 62; but *no permanent victory can be promised* 63; the goal of life: Calvin, Dante, Aristotle 63; the expulsion of final causes from nature 66; Hobbes on the death of the *summum bonum* 66; eternal happiness 66; Four maxims: *we should not accept any beliefs dogmatically*, etc. 67; *true religion is your own voice* 67; renouncing Tradition 68f.; and its objectionable 'block' view of religious truth 68; rejecting the old Western view of faith 68; true religion is an overflowing joy in life 70. Wordsworth 72; on ordinariness 72; on *bildung* 72; his emotivism 72; Final discussion of the ways in which culture turns biological feelings into universal religious feeling 75ff.; vertigo and the sublime 75; reading a picture 75; emptying out the self 76; world-love 76; vigilance 77.

Conclusion: modern society's great need of a (non-realist) spiritual discipline. We cannot do without it.

Notes	79
A Note about Books	83
Index of Names	84

The Way to Happiness

There have been many different theories of religion, and one of the main reasons why they have differed so much from one another is that they were framed to answer different questions. Georges Bataille's interesting theory suggests that we should see a society's religion as its way of 'blueing in' — wasting, sending up into the blue — its economic surplus.[1] Hence the extravagance and excess characteristic of many great religious occasions and monuments, from potlatches to multiple sacrifices and from Beauvais to Borobudur; and I think Bataille's theory does indeed illuminate much in the religious systems of the past. Their aggressive anti-utilitarianism, their furious expenditure, belong to a time when people did not assume, as we do, that any surplus should be reinvested. They just gave it back to their gods as generously as they had been given it. However, I am proposing an entirely different theory here, because I am looking for an answer to an entirely different question: How should we see religion for ourselves, today? I am aware of being a religious person: such a person has to wonder what kind of religion, with what kind of rationale, is possible for us now?

樂 樂 樂 樂 樂

We are not here dealing with Bataille's question and his answer, nor are we tackling the questions I dealt with in *After God* (1996). There I was talking about the history of God, the gods, and the supernatural world: God as the supreme author/authority, God as the awakener of our human consciousness, 'God' as the keystone of the whole world of linguistic meaning. I was interested in the public significance of the idea of God, and its strange historical development. But none of that is our present concern.

I need to produce a theory of religion because in 1999 I introduced a new method of religious enquiry. Troubled by the glaring irrationality of most religious belief, and the sheer disingenuousness of most apologetics,

I decided to take up an idea from Wittgenstein and try to find out what philosophical and religious ideas belong to all of us because they are built into the ordinary language that we all share. If I could map out this common ground, I would have a secure and democratic starting point for the religious and philosophical thought of the future. So I began to collect likely sounding idioms from the media, from dictionaries, from friends, and from memory.

It soon became clear that the material available is abundant indeed. Ordinary colloquial language uses a small vocabulary of only a few thousand words, but just one short but philosophically-evocative word of it — a word such as **life** (plus **live, living**), or **time** (plus **times, days, hours, moments, age**), or **see** (plus **seeing, blind**) — just a single word, taken together with a few others closely related, may have a cluster of over five hundred familiar and striking idiomatic phrases associated with it. Taking up the phrases that are the most provocative and that incorporate the boldest metaphors, and therefore cry out most insistently for analysis and interpretation, we start to unpack them. It turns out that they often make complex philosophical points in a nutshell. If we then take the obvious next step and start trying to date the idioms, we soon find that not only are we uncovering for the first time the subtle and complex metaphysics of ordinariness, but that we are also tracking its historical development, because so many of the idioms appear to be of very recent origin.

Ordinary language has always had its own rich philosophy built into it. To take a simple example, beautiful and puzzling phrases such as **It is cold** and **It came to pass** are almost as old as the English language. They go back deep into premodern times. If we were to collect enough of them, it would be quite easy for us to reconstruct the popular philosophy of the later medieval period. But during the past three generations or so there has been a rapid expansion of the media. We have become super-communicative, and as a result there has been an explosively rapid increase both in the number of stock phrases in the language, and in the rate of philosophical and religious change. The traditional ordinary-language world view changed very little between the ninth and the fifteenth centuries, but today I find that considerable changes have taken place just in my own lifetime. Hence the great excitement of unravelling for the first time, and recognizing the lineaments of, a great revolution in thought that has been and still is taking place within oneself and all one's millions of contemporaries.

To cut a long story short, my collection of idioms grew and I began to look for patterns and clues in it. I had the idea of highlighting what appeared to be the keywords that recurred most often. A count in my material showed that they were **life** and **it all**. I set **it all** aside for a while and concentrated upon **life**. When I had my first hundred life-idioms I looked for them in the *Shorter Oxford English Dictionary*, edition of 1972. Only one was there: the turn to **life** was apparently modern, very recent. I set about looking for ways of dating my life-idioms, and began the job of constructing an historical story about what has been happening to the word 'life' in the whole modern period — roughly, since Shakespeare. It was easy to buttonhole and to question friends who are highly expert both in the history of ideas and in the history of the English language. Bits at least of my argument were already familiar to some of them through their knowledge of writers such as Nietzsche and Lawrence.

The rest was plain sailing, and I don't need to do more here than recall some of the main theses of the little book that resulted.[2]

First, we have supposed that what has been happening during the past two centuries or so has been the secularization of religion; but we might more accurately describe it as the sacralization of life.

Second, in considerable detail the things that used to be said about God have today been rephrased as idioms about **life**. Some vivid examples demonstrate the point neatly: We say that one shouldn't **tempt life, deny life**, or **sin against life**. Sometimes we find ourselves joyfully **grateful to life**; in more testing times we may speak of ourselves as **wrestling with life**. I rest my case: **life** is undeniably the new religious object, at least so far as ordinary language is concerned.

Third, then, such idioms make my point and show that 'ordinary language is the best radical theologian'; in ordinary language we have to a considerable extent already gone over to a new this-wordly religion of ordinary human life. We have developed a 'kingdom-religion' of arrival and joy in life, and we are much less inclined nowadays to see ourselves as *in via*, on the road, marching towards a promised land after death or in the far future, than were our forebears.

Fourth, and last, Cupitt's notorious radical theology turns out to be the merest common sense, for our language proves that it is no more than what we all of us already believe and practise every day. And that is true even of the religious ultraconservatives who are my most vehement critics. They have failed to notice that they daily convict themselves out of their own mouths.

What about the philosophy that is built into ordinary language? Nobody has yet done all the studies of particular words that need to be done to answer this question adequately, but I have done a few. Recently I looked, for example, at **believe, belief**, and **have faith in**. I found that in ordinary language **to believe in** something is simply to accept it as genuine or as real, to **stand by** it, and to rely upon it; and **faith in** is trust. The intellectualist, or propositional, interpretation of belief and faith that is typical of the philosophical tradition — and therefore also of theology — is quite absent from ordinary language. In a word, the philosophy that is in ordinary language today is much closer in spirit to Heidegger and to pragmatism than it is to the main platonic tradition.

Such in brief were the ideas I first broached long ago in 1999, and then developed further in two little companion books during 2000, and in a philosophy of life in 2002 (published 2003).[3] The new method of religious enquiry involves a certain amount of empirical research, but it is not difficult to do because ordinary language is a topic on which every native English speaker is an expert. One consults dictionaries, the media, and friends, and one uses one's own wits. Even in the case of the more difficult words like **it** and **time**, where the number of good idioms is very large indeed, one should be reasonably confident of having gathered most of the relevant material within a few days. (**It** took me a few weeks. **It** was tough.) Then one gets down to classifying the material, not in the ways in which lexicographers classify it, but in terms of the philosophical and religious implications of it. Soon one begins, with a small shock of recognition, to grasp how ordinary language sees this particular matter. Then we need to look for exceptions, odd corners of usage, and the points upon which ordinary language is happy to incorporate conflicting opinions — the point here being that just as popular culture is often happy to incorporate conflicting proverbs into its stock, so ordinary language is not rigorously systematic in its philosophy, but at a number of points prefers to encourage the continuance of classical debates between conflicting views. It evidently feels in such a case that both views deserve to survive.

The new method of religious enquiry is empirical — so much so, indeed, that it is almost scientific. Anybody can check my whole argument out, bit by bit, for herself. And it seems to lead to very important conclusions, for by using the method we can demonstrate in detail a huge amount of common ground — the religion we all of us *really* believe in, the true *consensus fidelium*. But the first book fell dead-born from the press. Hardly anybody was interested. The unsophisticated are simply not used to thinking about religion in such a queer, novel way: for them religion is and must remain authoritative, traditional, brand-labelled, scriptural, *Christian*. The sophisticated suspected that there must be something wrong with an argument and a method that seem to claim that by a fairly simple empirical investigation we can quickly establish really important religious truths that we must and already do believe in, but don't yet know we believe in. 'Can this be right?' they wondered.

I am suggesting that the general silence and incredulity indicates that I need to embed my method of religious enquiry in a new theory of religion that will make it seem more clear, and more plausible. And that is why I need to produce a general theory of religion (and language, and community), if I am to overcome the doubts.

樂 樂 樂 樂 樂

The new theory of religion will differ (and has to differ) significantly from what we are used to. Until only a lifetime ago existence for the vast majority of human beings was almost inexpressibly harsh and laborious. People were horribly oppressed by physical necessity and by the violence of their masters. How did they endure it? In their situation it was entirely natural that they should make a sharp distinction between the way the world is and the way it ought to be, between nature and morality, description and evaluation. Their religions and ideologies tended to picture both a past and a future Age of Gold, so that they could say to themselves: 'Once, things were as they should be. But then we fell from grace, and the present wretched conditions of life ensued. But if we stick it out and keep the rules, we may hope to see Paradise restored, either at the end of time on this earth, or in the heavenly world after death.' So they lived between the memory of Paradise lost and the hope of Paradise regained: religion and art were dominated by hugely powerful and consoling images of an ideal world.

In its day, this old outlook seemed to make sense and helped people to endure their lives. We were astoundingly ignorant until two centuries or so ago, and still had no worthwhile theories about the processes of natural development through which things have come to be as they presently are. People had little or no idea that it was within their power considerably to improve the conditions of life during the present age. 'This world' had a bad name, and people did not expect sustained happiness in this life.

Our situation today is quite different and (in many ways, with deep regret) I have to say that it is time to say farewell to religion of the type that lived suspended between memory and hope. It appears that there was no Golden Age in the past, and there will not be one in the future. For us the gap between Is and Ought, the actual world and the ideal world, is much less wide than it used to be. We no longer have to put up with the severe social discipline of the past: that is why there has been such a welcome changeover from repression to free expression, and from morality to **lifestyle**. We should rejoice at the death of 'morality' — a hideous tyrant, especially over women. For us, the gap between the way things are and the way we would wish them to be is narrower than it formerly was. We no longer have such a great need to make our lives endurable by hoping that one day we'll see a world in which things are radically better than they are now. On the contrary, the longer we live the more we are inclined to reject dreams of redesigning the world. Instead, we prefer to love and accept and affirm things just as they are. Once we have achieved a modest sufficiency, civil peace, and a full span of life, that is about it. There is no more. There's nobody above us to complain to, and not very much to complain about, frankly. We should now see religion, not as a way of preparing for a better world, but as a symbolic language with which we voice our joy in and love for the world, life, and each other. The old pessimism can be forgotten.

At the University of Oxford, the theology syllabus used to be summarized in the mocking phrase, 'Eden to Chalcedon'. To acquire authority in matters of religion you needed to know three ancient languages and to put in some years of intensive study of the Old Testament, the New Testament, early church history, and the history of early Christian doctrine to AD 451. Nothing you really need to know about has happened since that date: such was the view. But I genuinely am saying, at last and with some reluctance, that it is now time to say farewell to religion based on holding supernatural beliefs about founding events in the remote past, recorded in sacred texts and certified to us by religious authority.[4] That whole way of thinking is now at an end. In philosophy, religion, and ethics it is better to think and act as if only the present, the here and now, really exists. We should not draw cheques upon the past, or the future, or tradition, or authority, because they will not be honoured.

樂 樂 樂 樂 樂

I have spoken of the regret and reluctance with which I abandon religion that appeals to a sacred, founding person and past chain of events, because, of course, what I am saying implies that Christianity cannot any longer stake everything on the truth of certain historical claims — claims about the incarnation of God the Son in Jesus Christ, about his personal character and his teaching, and about his death and his resurrection from the dead. This is partly because our whole culture is no longer tradition-directed: all our achievements since the rise of modern science and technology have been made possible by our being systematically sceptical about tradition. When was tradition ever demonstrably right about anything whatever? Is it not tradition that still keeps two-thirds of the human race in poverty, backwardness, and moral squalor? So far, we have usually tried to exempt our religion from the general scepticism about tradition, but, of course, the fact is that religion is above all the field where human beings are immiserated by their own obstinate loyalty to tradition. It is a fact that the quickest way to make most human beings, and especially female ones, happier would be simply to forget all traditional religion.

Fortunately, we in the West are throwing off tradition, but the other reason why Christianity needs to place less reliance on its traditional historical claims about Jesus Christ is that we now see that we don't know, and are never likely to know, enough about him to justify such claims or even to frame an agreed picture of him.[5]

Such evidence as we have about Jesus is almost all spin, with very little hard fact. It is damaged, fragmentary, and diverse, so that several different accounts of him are currently before the public, with little likelihood that one of them will prevail and drive out the others. The principal theories of Jesus — or, if you prefer, some principal theories — are those of orthodoxy, of 'consistent eschatology', and of the Jesus Seminar. The orthodox one regards the portrait of him given in the synoptic Gospels of Matthew, Mark, and Luke as substantially accurate, and sees him as a claimant-Messiah whose followers gradually recognized in him a more-than-metaphorical divine Sonship. The 'consistent-eschatology' account derives from Holzmann's recognition in the late nineteenth century of the priority of Mark's Gospel, and was classically set out by Johannes Weiss and Albert Schweitzer.[6] It sees in Jesus a prophet of the violent arrival of the Kingdom of God, who set his face towards Jerusalem in the hope of forcing the issue, and then found as he was dying that he was not going to be vindicated. His followers' continuing hope that they might yet see him return in glory was gradually transformed into the orthodox theology. Thirdly, the Jesus Seminar account argues that the earliest Gospels (Q,Ur-Thomas) were simply sayings-collections, like the Dhammapada. Jesus had been an almost secular teacher of wisdom. His biography (including the passion narrative) is just about entirely mythical, reflecting the complex process by which he was gradually turned into a world saviour, a divine Redeemer. This process, the narrative apotheosis of someone who was originally just a teacher, is a little like what happened in the case of the Buddha.[7]

These three accounts of Jesus differ widely from one another, but the available evidence is such that each of them can be made plausible when presented by a skilled advocate, and it is not likely that we will ever decide that one of them is straightforwardly right, and the others are wrong. On the contrary, all the indications are that the uncertainty and the ambiguity will persist indefinitely. The original Jesus eludes us: his culture and ways of thinking are too remote. He is inexorably slipping away from us forever, just as the other great figures of classical antiquity are slipping away from us, and just as, for example, Shakespeare is very slowly slipping away and ceasing to be revivable as popular theatre. Much as we may deplore this, it happens. Already it has to be admitted that there is very little writing earlier than Jane Austen that needs no help because it spontaneously revives itself.

Personally I retain a strong devotion to Jesus, and I sympathize with the saying of Nikos Kazantzakis that there have been just three great teachers of humanity, namely the Buddha, Jesus, and Nietzsche. But we cannot any longer make our whole ethic and philosophy of life logically dependent, either upon the personal authority of a great figure from the classical past or upon the truth of historical claims about such a figure.

❀ ❀ ❀ ❀ ❀

I have suggested instead that the religious thought of the future should talk as if **only the present exists**— not a bad maxim for one's shaving-mirror — and should assume as standard a cultural situation in which the great mass of people has already achieved a modest sufficiency, civil peace and a full span of life. Such people are, of course, still exposed and subject to time, accident and death — temporality, contingency, and finitude. But they have learnt enough wisdom to know that we should give up bitter complaining and instead love life and say Yes to life just as it is. It is people like these whom we should have in mind. What can religion be for them?

❀ ❀ ❀ ❀ ❀

It will soon be apparent that the theory of religion proposed here is closer in spirit to the traditional ascetical theology than to either dogmatic or systematic theology. The latter is chiefly concerned with justifying and magnifying the power and claims of the Church, a cause that does not concern me at all. But I am interested in making sense of the religious life, and of spirituality as religious style — not least, in relation to modern ideas of personality development. Today, when average life expectancy has already increased so greatly and is likely to increase still further, it is not surprising that everyone is becoming aware of having a personal religious history that has led her through a series of stages over the years. Inevitably, the passage of time tends to disillusion us, as we become aware of **seeing through** beliefs and opinions that only a few years ago seemed to us solid and convincing. This **seeing through** goes on and on: where is it leading us?

❀ ❀ ❀ ❀ ❀

For a first sketch of the theory of religion, I raise the question: When does the ordinary person today use religious language, speaking spontaneously and uninhibitedly about God, about Jesus and Christ, and about Hell and damnation? Answer: This vocabulary is used in profanities, about which two things need to be said at once. One is that our profanities are genuinely religious uses of distinctively religious terms. Sometimes the words being used are veiled, by euphemism or periphrasis or whatever, as when people say **Goodness!** instead of **God!**, **Gor blimey!** instead of **God blind me!**, and **Bloody** instead of **By our Lady!** But nowadays, God, Jesus, and Christ are used baldly, because the original point of swearing was to add force to what was being said by invoking God as your witness. There is a certain frisson, a certain excitement and danger, in calling upon God or Christ in this way; and the frisson tends to be transferred from the profane word itself to the strong cosmic feeling that one is seeking to express. This means that the profanity — just **God!** perhaps — itself calls up, shares with others, focusses, channels, and discharges the cosmic feeling of awe, of frustration, of horror, of gratitude, or perhaps even of relief, that is involved. Thus my second point about profanity is that it is an expressive use of religious language to pour out cosmic feeling — an outpouring that is often by only a hairsbreadth different from prayer. Suppose that you turn a corner on a hill walk and suddenly confront a magnificent view. You stop, and breathe: **Oh, God!** Suppose you pick up the telephone and are abruptly told tragic news about an old and dear friend. **Oh God!** you say. Suppose that once again you are blocked at work in your attempt to gain something to which you are entitled. Indignantly, you snort: **Oh, God!** Now make up a few more such examples, and then ask yourself, 'Which of these are cases of true prayer, and which are cases of sinful swearing that take God's name in vain?' It is often hard to say.

The first sketch of our theory of religion is then as follows: in religious practice, the distinctive vocabulary of religion is used to arouse, gather, focus, channel, and discharge strong cosmic feeling. Such practice may be individual and private, or it may be public and communal; and the feelings involved may be of many, many different kinds. What makes the feeling 'cosmic' is its strength, and the fact that it is not fixated or locked on to a particular, finite object. It is universal and, as yet, unfocussed feeling.

To follow up a topic raised earlier, suppose that on a fine morning the world looks good and I feel good. More than that, I feel grateful, but not grateful to any particular benefactor. If I am a slightly old-fashioned person, I may say, **Thank God!** If I am a more modern person, I may declare that on a day like this **I feel grateful to life**. I don't thank life itself, aloud, and surely nobody really personifies life in that way; but by declaring myself grateful to life I am enabled after a fashion to voice my strong, cosmic, objectless feeling of gratitude. My father, reaching the age of 80 in excellent health, made a similar point by saying simply, **I've been lucky**, meaning: 'There's no reason for it, and I can't say I deserve it, but I'm fortunate, I'm blessed, and I acknowledge the fact'.

Developing this theme a stage further, we may see a church service, a piece of well-constructed liturgy, as a sort of emotional music. Successive items of the service, performing different speech-acts, conjure up and discharge a logically and dramatically ordered and intelligible sequence of feelings. Until the Baroque period, and perhaps even a little later, there was a rich Latin vocabulary for the various ritual actions and speech-acts that are used in prayer and in public worship, but it is now almost forgotten, and one does not often 'assist at' a well-composed act of worship. But when worship is properly made, it is just the same as theatre – except that we are all of us on stage. And its religious validity is of course quite independent of the (realistically assessed or 'objective') truth of the various theological beliefs that seem to be presupposed. Indeed, objective truth is irrelevant and unimportant in such a case.

Do you see what I mean? I mean to make the very obvious point that an act of thanksgiving, in the form perhaps of a hymn, expresses a cosmic feeling of objectless gratitude for blessings received that does not in fact depend upon there being someone out there who is gratified by our effusive gratitude to Him. In fact, the realistic analysis of what is going on in public worship is (as we shall see) a vulgar misinterpretation of the situation; but unfortunately our religious leaders regard a paganising and idolatrous realism as being compulsory in these matters.

We leave this stage of the argument with the cheerful images of a church as a theatre that is all stage and no auditorium and of worship as a sort of communal swearing session that makes us all feel a lot better afterwards. We turn now to the related question of obscenities. How do they differ from profanities? How is it that I can plausibly represent profanity as close to prayer, but that obscenities — despite the best efforts of D.H. Lawrence — remain obstinately taboo, and at the opposite pole from prayers? Certainly it is true that there is a long tradition in Christianity, in Hinduism, and even in Sufism, of using quite bold sexual metaphors in religion and of using religious language in sex; but religion does not try to adopt and baptize the semi-taboo vocabulary of popular sexual words, which remain flavoured with a touch, or more than a touch, of somewhat ugly aggression and contempt. Yet the obscenities do raise a question for my theory of religion, for this vocabulary also calls up, focusses, channels, and discharges strong feeling. The way the obscenities work is, in short, somewhat like the way the major religious words work. *What's the difference*, and *why*?

Briefly, the answer is this: In males, especially, the sexual impulse is highly 'convergent'. It doesn't go out into 'cosmic' objectlessness. It isn't linked with self-surrender. On the contrary, it goes straight for object-choice: it fixes upon and takes possession of its (finite) object. It is associated with pride, self-affirmation, and conquest. So the natural movement, at least of the male sex drive, is in the opposite direction from religion. The female sexual impulse, on the other hand, has always been thought somewhat closer to religion because of its strong element of self-surrender and oceanic feeling. However, society recognizes the potential threat that there is in male sexual aggression, and accordingly makes object-choice even more important to women than it is to men. Because the woman risks more, she must be allowed and encouraged to be as choosy as she wishes. Society must underwrite her entire freedom to choose the person to whom she wishes to give herself. But the consequence of this is that the resemblance between female sexual feeling and religion holds only in the case of the more realistic sort of piety that objectifies and personifies the gods. If non-realism is correct, and the religious object is not another person out there with whom I fall in love and to whom I want to surrender myself, then there is not a close affinity between religious devotion and female sexuality. On the contrary, religious devotion should be seen in rather more Buddhist terms, as a passing-out into cool, empty beatitude rather than as erotic ecstasy. If so, then obscenities should be seen as revealing something of the dark side of sex and no doubt as being interesting and important to us just as such, but not as being of religious significance.

※ ※ ※ ※ ※

Bataille's theory suggests that the distinctive shape of a society's religion was given by the way it burnt up, wasted, or 'skied' its economic surplus. To that I have in effect replied that nowadays we are all prudent protestants who consider that we should not waste but reinvest our economic surplus. However, Bataille's influence has come through after all, because I have suggested that our religion supplies us with a vocabulary — liturgical, ethical, etc. — through which we can expend our emotional surplus.

I am not sure that we differ from other animals in being much more rational than they are. Rather, it seems to me that we differ from other animals in the excessive strength of our feelings both of joy and of depression, both of owed gratitude and of horror and dread. We struggle to discharge the excess through various symbolic outlets: games, art, religion, gardening, or even (in my own misfortunate case) thought.

※ ※ ※ ※ ※

An interesting sidelight on the theme (on page 12 above) of liturgy as a complex emotional drama composed of a chain of distinct ritual acts is given by a scarce and valuable book, F.E. Brightman's edition (1903) of *The Preces Privatae of Lancelot Andrewes*.[8] Andrewes (1555–1626) had considerable classical learning, and made a complex theatre even of his private prayers, morning and evening, daily. He was not the sort of man who would ever muddle his comprecations, imprecations, and deprecations, and each step in the series of ritual acts is headed with its correct label.

In more recent times we have almost wholly lost the knowledge of how to structure private prayers in a series of *acta* that follow an established dramatic order — a good example, by the way, of the fact that much or most of Christianity has already been lost, even by believers. The most any reader of these words is likely to have been taught is that one should follow the order summarized by the acronym ACTS (adoration, confession, thanksgiving, supplication). But the old formality of someone like Andrewes shows that before the fall into modern, naïve religious realism took place, people instinctively understood religion in emotive-expressive, speech-act, and dramatic terms.

The old vocabulary, I should add, was of pre-Christian origin. The pagan Romans were a fussy lot, who had a very nice and exact notion of how temple rituals should be constructed. They bequeathed their rich vocabulary to the infant Latin Church.

❈ ❈ ❈ ❈ ❈

Religion is cosmic emotion, I have suggested. Our feelings quickly become much too strong for the finite setting in which they have arisen, and spill over to become cosmic feelings, feelings about **It All**. Whether in profanity or in prayers, religious language typically attracts, focusses, channels, and gives expression to cosmic feeling — and we feel better for having got **It All** off our chests.

We are made of feelings, and when our feeling-life flows most strongly and is able easily to find satisfying expression, we are happy. So the goal or *telos* of religion is simply happiness — cosmic happiness, or eternal happiness. *Cosmic happiness* is happiness about **It All**, general, all-round happiness about **It all**, and about our own place in **It All**. We feel easy, or as I often put it **easy, going**, because we are content to accept universal transience and our own transience as parts of **It All**.

Eternal happiness also needs to be defined. We are not here talking about eternity in the sense of timelessness: we are using eternal in the nineteenth-century and post-Platonic sense. *Eternal happiness* is a kind of happiness that can be relied upon not to leave us, however bad things get to be for us. The old scriptural phrase for it was joy in affliction (2 Cor 7:4, KJV and RV). Today one may hear people speak of 'inner peace'.

In summary, cosmic and eternal happiness is religious happiness, and is my purely this-worldly version of what used to be called beatitude. We have only this life, and in this life we remain subject to the traditional forms of metaphysical evil — contingency, temporality, and finitude, or more simply chance, time, and death. We will therefore never know completely unmixed happiness: there is no such thing. But we can know eternal happiness in the sense of joy in affliction, and, believe me, that is not a little thing. (In fact, I think it's better than Heaven ever was.)

樂 樂 樂 樂 樂

It is now time to broach the question of the religious object — an important matter because we are going to show that when for the first time in our lives we approach the question of God in a way that gives its due priority to ordinary language, everything is transformed. We perceive with astonishment that we have all of us been badly mishandling the word 'God' for a very, very long time.

The mistake? We have been treating God as a theory in speculative metaphysics that is proposed to explain why something exists rather than nothing, how the world began, why we have the world we have and not some other world, and how we are to find a really firm dogmatic starting point for all thought about the world and the human condition and about Truth and Goodness. We have been thinking of God as a being out there, and picturing orthodox theism as a golden mean between deism (which is too dry) and pantheism (which is too wet and fuzzy). So satisfactory have we supposed this formulation to be that we think everyone can be classified conveniently as being either a theist, an agnostic, or an atheist — and when that point is settled, the most important of the great questions of life have been dealt with.

This whole way of thinking is very badly wrong, in ways that attention to ordinary language will soon make clear. But it needs to be emphasized that, despite the best efforts of professional linguists and of philosophers such as Wittgenstein, we still do not clearly understand either the workings or the world view of ordinary language, and there is still no satisfactory account of the philosophy that is in ordinary language. From the point of view of philosophy, the world of ordinary language remains largely unknown.

Back in 1959, when Iona and Peter Opie published *The Lore and Language of Schoolchildren* (Oxford: the Clarendon Press) the authors remarked upon the strangeness of their position. They had written the first substantial book about a whole fascinating and enchanted world, a world that is right under our noses, and which every one of us actually lived in between the ages of about six and fourteen — but a world that we have for many years neglected and forgotten. My task here is much stranger even than that, because the world of ordinary language is much closer to us than the world of our own childhood, and yet remains unknown to us. The reason for this is that, at least since Plato, ordinary language's ways of thinking have been regarded as low, confused, and simply mistaken. Education has always been a training in the rejection of ordinary ways of thinking and in the adoption of more lucid 'platonic' ideas about theory, reason, generality, understanding, and so on. Education has always attempted systematically to alienate us from the ordinariness in which we all began, and upon which everything still rests.

I'm not going to describe here the pathology that results from all this. Nor need I do more than briefly recall that Western thought began to discover ordinariness towards the end of the eighteenth century, with the first philosophical attention to the motion of living — as distinct from dead — languages, and with the collection of items from popular culture such as sagas, ballads, and fairy tales. Interest in the life and the 'condition' of the common people on the part of social investigators, parliamentary committees, revolutionary socialists and novelists followed, and the state gradually assumed fuller responsibility for measuring and managing the numbers, the health, the education, and the general welfare of the people. But the notion that the thought of ordinary people might be intellectually interesting, and might have a logic of its own quite different from the 'academic' or 'platonic' style of thinking traditional in the high culture of the West, developed only very slowly. So far as it has yet come in at all, it has come in via anthropology. By this I mean the suggestion that if we can grasp the idea that tribespeople in the Amazon basin may have ways of thinking of their own, different from ours but nevertheless genuinely interesting, then we may be able to grasp the idea that ordinariness in our own society similarly has a world of thought of its own that does make sense in its own terms, even if it may seem strange to us. To this, psychoanalysis added the further suggestion that we may need to recognize that an exotic world that is even closer to us than the world of childhood, namely the world of ordinary language, may still be functioning inside our own heads. We are still in it. You may prefer to think of yourself as having been thoroughly civilized (i.e., platonized) by education, but you may need to recognize in your dreams, your fantasies, and your psychological troubles something else, something old and important, still surviving within yourself but which has for too long been neglected.

Considerations such as these have gradually prepared us for the revolutionary idea that there really is an interesting philosophy and set of ways of thinking embedded in ordinary language, and that it is about time for us to dig it all out and take a good look at it. When post-Nietzschean philosophers such as Wittgenstein, Dewey, and Heidegger came along, telling us that we must now learn to think in a post-Platonic, post-metaphysical way, then clearly the time had come for the philosophy that is in ordinariness to emerge. But, even at this late date, it is proving a difficult birth. Really, *very* difficult — and nowhere more so than in the philosophy of religion.

樂 樂 樂 樂 樂

What then of God in ordinary language? One's first impulse is to collect the God-idioms, as I did in *The Meaning of It All in Everyday Speech* (London: SCM Press, 1999), p.50. In that first investigation I found some twenty. Today I would be willing to add seven more items, as follows:

> **Put the fear of God into**
> **God does exist after all!** (said on hearing of an opponent's misfortune)
> **God-forsaken**
> **God bless!**
> **God grant**
> **In the lap of the gods**
> **Playing God**

But these additional items do not cause me to modify my earlier conclusion that this is a disappointingly short list, lacking in quality. No items in it are both new and interesting: most items are mere relics of the faith of the past, or expletives, or mocking and ironical. What has been lost is the fact that there was once a time when the whole gamut of human emotion found expression in and through the relation to God. Where has all that wealth and variety gone?

The answer is given by the same little book. The full emotional range is today to be found in the it-idioms; and not only the it-idioms, because (as I recall having first noticed towards the end of the 1980s) there is a whole group of terms that we now use in quasi-theological ways. They are — at least — **things, everything, it, it all, life,** and sometimes also **existence** and **being.**

We use these general expressions to symbolize what we are in the midst of, what we are up against, and what we have to deal with. We are talking about something general, encircling, and nonhuman that imposes upon us the conditions to which we are subject and deals out to us our fate. We are talking here about the not-self generally; about our life's Other. What we are talking about is what you are asking about when you enquire sympathetically of a friend: **How's it all going? How's everything with you? How are things? How is it with you? How's life?** And I hope by now you are beginning yourself to produce more phrases like these; indeed, I hope that your spine is tingling by now as you begin to appreci-

ate the numinous and alarming theological overtones that accompany so
many seemingly innocuous and euphemistic expressions in ordinary language.

What we are talking about here, the encircling **It All**, sometimes
seems implacable. **It** has all the power, and we have none. When we are
in this mood, we may symbolize it as **Fate, destiny**, or **kismet**. At other
times **it** may strike us as rather capricious, and even as casually generous
and benign. We may hope it will take the heat off us and give us an easier
time. In this mood, we may speak of it as **Fortune, luck** or **chance**.
(Another associated word, potent in this connection, is the word **hap**,
together with its many interesting cognates: **mayhap, perhaps, happening, happiness**, etc.)[9]

Finally, we should mention the most powerful of all these quasi-theological words through which we still articulate our sense of the human
condition and our attempts to battle our way through it: the words **God**
and **life**. **God** was once the most powerful word of all, but many of the
ideas and feelings once articulated in God-talk are now transferred to
other words, and especially to the word **life**, which currently has, if not
the largest, then certainly the richest and most varied crowd of idioms
surrounding it.

Now we can set out the whole list of expressions for the religious
object in ordinary language. They are:

1 Things, everything, it, it all, existence, being
2 Fate, destiny, kismet
3 Fortune, luck, chance
4 God
5 Life

This list immediately makes it clear that ordinary language does not
operate with a metaphysical idea of God, does not privilege a realist view
of God, and is not even especially interested in the *word* God — nor in
what religious traditions usually call God's 'Name'. Particular religious
systems are usually most insistent upon the importance of calling upon
the right god by the right name, and using just the right ritual forms. They
demand exclusive brand loyalty. But ordinary language is simply not interested in any of that. In its view God currently happens to be simply a
rather out-of-fashion member of a whole cluster of vague words whose
respective behaviours and ranges of idiomatic use exhibit a strong family
resemblance. The various members of the cluster of about fourteen words
are used almost *ad lib*, and in a strikingly agnostic way. We just don't mind
whether the idiom we happen to use incorporates the term **it**, or **fate**, or
things. We are not interested in speculative theology, nor in describing

the 'nature' of the religious object. Our interest is in the individual person's battle through life. We ask **How has it all been for you, lately?** and we are not too curious about exactly what terms are used in the reply. There are various possible responses, for example:

Life was very hard for a time, but things are looking up now.
It all went pear-shaped at first, but you know what they say:
you have to make your own luck.

The last phrase reminds that not only do people not mind precisely what terms are used — you may **wrestle with God, wrestle with life**, or simply refuse to **let it get you down** — but also they freely take a non-realist view of the religious object. We may say that **life teaches us a lesson,** or that **life is hard on us**, but we also say anti-realist things like **life is what you make it** and **he's made life hard for himself.** We complain about our run of ill-luck, but then recollect ourselves and say that **we make our own luck.** When I have **got into a rut**, I often need to remind myself that the rut I'm stuck in is not a real rut-out-there, but merely a metaphor for my own bad habits, in which I'm stuck by my own laziness. I thought I was 'not a bus but a tram' — that is, I was inclined to think determinism true, and to picture myself as being on rails — but then somebody pointed out to me that we ourselves laid the track on which we seem to be running.

Ordinary language seems to be full of echoes of religion, full of vivid metaphors in which we picture **life** or **it** as a sort of *person* with whom we must negotiate. But on closer examination we realise that what ordinary language actually says *about* the religious object is very fluid and imprecise. It has no interest in speculative theology. All its interest is in the metaphorical enrichment of the individual person's religious sense of life, and in the daily ups and downs of our struggle through life.

樂 樂 樂 樂 樂

Here is another example of ordinary language's intensely practical orientation and its total lack of speculative curiosity. It relates to the question of **belief**, referred to earlier on page 4. A day spent collecting the ordinary-language belief-idioms makes it clear that when ordinary people raise questions of belief they are not doing so out of intellectual curiosity. Linked with the German *glaube* and with *lief*, **belief** is related to confidence, trust, and even love:

I believe in …
Self-belief, belief in oneself
Contrary to popular belief
I am of the belief that

Beyond belief
To the best of my belief
Believable, credible, credibility
I would never have believed it of him
'Four men are believed to be trapped in …'
Believe it or not
Believe you me / Believe me, it's well worth the effort
I don't believe in …
I'm a great believer in …
I could hardly believe my own luck
Don't you believe it / Would you believe it / You'd better believe it!
I was hardly able to believe my own eyes / believe my ears
Seeing is believing
Believe nothing of what you hear, and only half of what you see
I don't believe a word of it!

To this fairly short list of idioms and phrases, I add two amusing quotations that use **belief** in exactly the ordinary-language way:

It is so many years before one can believe enough in what one feels even to know what the feeling is.
(W.B. Yeats, *Autobiographies*)

He who believes in nothing still needs a girl to believe in him.
(Eugen Rosenstock-Huessy)[10]

The reader needs to go through the main list of twenty idioms and imagine the force of each in its own typical setting in actual use. It soon becomes clear that the use of 'Do you believe in God?' to mean 'Do you think that there is a God?' or 'Do you think that God exists?' is a special case that has arisen because of the history of 'God' in our culture. In the period of Christian culture (about 400–1700) atheism was rare and 'Do you believe in God?', if asked at all, would have been a question about your piety, not about your ontology and world view. But as faith in God faded, 'Do you believe in God?' gradually turned into a question about your views on a problematic entity that may or may not actually exist. And that is a very unhappy way of formulating an important question about religion.

Otherwise, and apart from this one special case, we find that ordinary language sticks close to the older usage which links 'belief' with 'lief', as in the phrase **I'd as lief**. Here, 'lief' refers to what I am comfortable with, familiar with, happy with. In ordinary language, belief is always a matter of personal confidence; it is a matter of knowing whom I can trust and what side to take. The happy state to live in, and the one we always seek, is the state of easy, unquestioning loyalty. I raise questions about belief when my usual state of untroubled confidence in some person, or cause, or perhaps remedy, has suddenly been shaken, and I urgently demand something that will restore my confidence. If you don't act quickly to put it right, there is a real likelihood that I'll suddenly have an abrupt moodswing and walk out. Then it will be very difficult to get me back, because within days I'll be developing new habits and new loyalties that will seal the breach forever.

So, if we wish to talk about questions of 'faith' and 'belief' as they affect ordinary people, we would do well to look at specific cases. How, for example, does it sometimes come about that the public loses confidence in the safety of a particular medical treatment for babies, or a particular food, or a particular technology; and by what means do politicians, companies, and others set about rebuilding public confidence?

樂 樂 樂 樂 樂

I hope that by now we are becoming clearer about the connections between the new method of religious enquiry (by collecting idioms and reconstructing the developing worldview that belongs to us all because it is built into ordinary language) and the new theory of religion. As the case of **belief** showed, in ordinary language 'belief' is not intellectualist belief that x or y is the case. It is not a matter of weighing probable evidence, nor is it an involuntary 'finding' that one assents to a proposition presented to and entertained in the mind. Belief is entirely a matter of whom and what I daily trust. It is a matter of personal acceptance, allegiance, going-along-with, trust, endorsement and reliance. To all of us humans, what matters first and most of all is the matter of finding out who and what we can trust and go along with in our daily struggle through life. And in this context I am thinking of religion as a way of producing and maintaining high morale; as a way of summoning up and celebrating our joy and trust in the world, in life, and in each other.

In the late-modern world, it is precisely that existential confidence (**What's the point of it all? What's it all about? Is it all worthwhile?**) that is so often felt to be fragile and in need of boosting. Our chronic liability to unhappiness is linked with our liability to crises of confidence, and both are symptoms of a religious problem.

樂 樂 樂 樂 樂

Before I die I'd like to be able to say that I have looked coolly at the plain, unvarnished truth of the human condition, without feeling any fear, or impulse to complain, or need for protective illusions. Better still, I'd like to be able to describe such an outlook in a text, and to say that, even against such a background, a religious love of and gratitude for the world, and life, and each other are still possible and do make sense as a basis upon which to live and to feel that life is worthwhile.

In short, I still cling to my old, crazy ambition: I'd like to write a book that is both religious and truthful. (It will be the first, or almost the first, such book, if and when someone actually produces it.) Can we imagine this ambition being achieved within the framework and the vocabulary here being set out? Let us now take the exposition of our theory of religion one spit deeper.

I have been saying — what is obvious enough — that ordinary language is unlike Platonism because it is not oriented towards metaphysics and therefore does not attach supreme value to theoretical or contemplative knowledge. Ordinary language grew up to facilitate our social intercourse and our cooperation in the human world: that is almost all that ordinary language cares about, but not *quite* all, for ordinary language does have, and often voices, a perfectly genuine cognitive interest of its own. It wants to know, and we all want to know, **What it's all about**. In a troubled mood, we look for a vocabulary that will help us to cope with, to understand, and to accept our common human condition. **What's it all supposed to mean? What does it all add up to?** When in phrases like these — there are hundreds of them — we invoke **It All**, or **It**, or **Things**, or **Everything**, or **Being**, or **Existence**, or **Life** we are talking about the sum of all the conditions and circumstances that encircle our lives. These circumstances, and many of the conditions, are variable. Sometimes **things go well for us**, whereas at other times **things go badly for us**. Why the variation? Can we find some way of negotiating with or influencing **it all**, and so stabilizing our existence somewhat?

I am suggesting that religion is our way, both communal and individual, of 1) expressing our feelings about It All; 2) totalizing and *thinking* **It All**; and 3) dealing or doing business with **It All**. Of these three, 1) finding a vocabulary in which one can express cosmic feeling, is closest to poetry; 2) finding a speculative language in which one can theorize and try to explain the human condition is closest to philosophy; 3) doing business with **It All** in the hope thereby of improving our own lot is closest to ritual and (nowadays) technology.

Of these three, we can certainly have some success with 1), but 2) and 3) are more problematical. Given what I have been saying about ordinary language and its typical ways of thinking, how can we hope to find a non-metaphysical way of totalizing and interpreting **It All**?

The answer I propose is this: platonic or 'academic' understanding is ideal, dispassionate, and theoretical. It is closer to philosophy. But ordinary language, as one can soon learn by studying the behaviour and the idioms of words like **truth**, **faith**, and **belief**, is invariably and instinctively religious. Without any hesitation, it goes straight for an engaged, committed, self-involving, and quite unspeculative kind of understanding. Obviously it can never hope and would never attempt to totalize **It All** theoretically, in Hegel's way. No, ordinary language can only totalize **It All** by experiencing and describing its overall impact upon me. It is unified in the way we are prompted by it to feel about it, and is brought to life by the metaphors in which we try to articulate our response to it. Inevitably, the most vivid and striking of these metaphors have tended to picture **the nature of things**, **It All**, as some kind of superperson, with whom we 'wrestle', and whom eventually we may learn to trust and even to love. But today this language of wrestling, trusting, and loving has been largely transferred from **God** to **Life**, and is used in a consciously non-realist spirit. Of course it is we who have made the superperson that we speak about. To see this clearly, think of the very similar — indeed, closely related — case of 'the weather' or 'the climate'. The weather affects my mood, and I tend to respond by attributing some kind of disposition to the weather. It is mild, stormy, lovely, or harsh, according to the way it affects me; and one notices that it-idioms have always been used of the weather in the English/Anglo-Saxon tradition. So we all speak in anthropomorphic language about the weather, and nobody minds; and, similarly, we all tend to speak in anthropomorphic language about **It All**, about **Fate**, about **Life**, and so on, and nobody should mind. The main consensus of English ordinary-language usage already shows that we have given up the idea that there is an existing quasi-personal God out there, and if and when we are agreed upon that point we can take a relaxed view of our anthropomorphic idioms.

樂 樂 樂 樂 樂

We need to consider how the religious vocabulary through which we might want to express ourselves today differs from the vocabulary used by our ancestors.

Classical Christianity, in both its Eastern and its Western forms, developed a rich vocabulary that was able to do several jobs at once — that is, it was able to evoke, to channel, and to discharge about five distinct and powerful feelings simultaneously. It sacralized and celebrated the social order, both in the church and in the state, and it focussed worship upon the supreme spiritual authority that held everything together, grounding the social order in the cosmic order, and both in the eternal will of God. It offered consoling, beautiful images of an ideal world beyond death to people whose lives in this world were harsh and (usually) unfulfilled. Above all, perhaps, it inspired the faithful with a touch of messianism — the feeling that they as a people were promised a glorious destiny that would surely be attained, one day.

Thus the weekly sung Liturgy called up and gave symbolic expression to a cluster of deeply held communal feelings: worship of the One in whom everything hangs together, veneration for the leaders of religious and civil society, yearning for a better world, the consciousness of being together with others on the march towards that better world, and finally — mixed up with all this — the weekly remembrance of and communion with one's own beloved dead. In Europe, for about fifteen centuries, all this was religion, and there are some people for whom some of it is still alive. But most of us now recognize that the epoch when there can be a great folk-church with an all-inclusive, sacred cosmology is long past and cannot be recovered. There is no likelihood at all of its reinstatement. Today's cosmology has irreversibly become scientific and secular, and the social order can no longer be grounded in the cosmic order in the old way. Our worldview depends upon a general consent that has to be worked for and renegotiated continuously — which means that in our world nothing is sacrosanct, and everything is permanently on the negotiating table. Society has become diverse, individually, ethnically, and religiously. The world has become just the human world, and this human life-world of ours has no outside and is in no way grounded in anything beyond itself. There is only us and **It All**: there is only **life**.

The permanent loss of grounding or 'foundations' leaves ordinary people troubled with a haunting sense of pointlessness and emptiness. This is a very serious matter; in fact, it is often **life-threatening**. In recent years it has been well portrayed in cinema films such as *American Beauty* and *The Hours*. In this situation the task of religion is not to find and to teach people old-style theoretical 'answers', because there aren't any, but to find ways of filling people with an intense religious (i.e., open and not fixated) love for life, for the world and for each other. People need to be filled with the conviction that **all this**, just as it is, can be blessed and can be enough for us.

Our modern ontology is parsimonious: there is only us, our language, our life, our world. There is therefore nothing anymore for religion to be except what I have elsewhere called 'solar ethics': true religion is joy in, and love for, and commitment to our life, our world, and each other. Being 'solar' involves forgetting the old yearning for a timeless world and instead learning to 'dance with the dream', being '**easy, going**' — i.e., relaxed about one's own transience, and accepting that we are passing away along with everything else.[11]

I am describing a religious mood and style that have given up the traditional 'grand narrative' of cosmic Fall and Redemption. Instead, everything's put in the present tense. So far as the question of evil is concerned, we shift the main emphasis from moral evil to metaphysical evil (which is, traditionally, the contingency, temporality, and finitude that cloud all life in this world, and have been wrongly alleged to make 'real' and lasting happiness unattainable here below). We overcome metaphysical evil by forcibly revaluing it and showing that we cannot really wish it away. For example, without temporality, how could there ever have been linguistic meaning, and how could there ever have been life, at all? Indeed, how could there ever be an *actual* world, as distinct from an ideal world-design, without contingency, temporality, and finitude? So instead of complaining, why not try affirming happenstance, time and death as being entirely acceptable conditions for the actualization of a world, the living of lives, and the production of values? Our worship will then be world-love, world-joy, solarity, and high spirits, and we'll try never to complain again. Never!

Elsewhere I have tried to demonstrate that an outlook very close to this one has, during the past few decades, arrived in what I might call the 'idiomatic' of ordinary language. This is what we are all coming to think and feel. And it is not simply a rejection and reversal of our main religious tradition, because in many ways it is a fulfilment of tradition. It can readily be seen as being the kingdom-religion to which our tradition has been looking forward since the days of the ancient Israelite prophets.

樂 樂 樂 樂 樂

Some people may wish to object to the ideas here being put forward, on the grounds that they are 'postmodern' (and therefore, supposedly, unsound and irrational), or Nietzschean (and therefore antireligious). Well, the philosophical issue here has been in continuous contestation for many years past, and no doubt will go on for many more years yet; and as for the religious issue, it is worth pointing out that like nearly all the great German philosophers Nietzsche was deeply influenced by Lutheranism, and always remained a person temperamentally religious, who had to have a gospel to preach. Indeed, from F.A. Lea to Alistair Kee there has never been a shortage of radical Christian readings of Nietzsche.[12] Furthermore, I should point out that I have never been a very loyal follower, either of Nietzsche or of anybody else, and have always refused to follow Nietzsche when he starts talking the aggressively tough language of right-wing evolutionary ethics. (And to do Nietzsche himself justice, he himself does not look for any following of loyalists. Zarathustra sends his disciples away, telling them not to follow him, but to follow themselves.[13])

❈ ❈ ❈ ❈ ❈

Suppose we are agreed that true religion now is to forget metaphysics and to forget any sort of concern for one's personal salvation. Instead one should *burn* with universal, non-fixated — even, deliberately nondiscriminating and nonselective — love for life, for our world, and for one's fellow human. Much traditional religion sought to escape from or to 'transcend' time, chance, and mortality; but I have argued that instead we should accept and affirm our own transience and pass joyfully away, along with everything else. Our Yes to life must include a Yes to life's temporality and finitude. We are not going to escape the common fate, so we should embrace it without regrets or complaints. As for the traditional Western Christian ethic of purifying one's soul and preparing for death, it was a complete waste of time (in txt msg spk, a CWOT). Life is outsideless, and there is nothing in death for which any kind of personal preparations can be made; and the ethic of fastidiously recoiling from others was a mistake too, for we live by mingling with our environment and with other human beings. A sealed, pure self with no immigration or emigration across its borders does not exist — and would be worthless even if it did exist. Forget purity!

Suppose then that we accept all this solar ethics: then what religious vocabulary and set of practices will best school us in it and help us to become easy and habitual in living it?

Some may wish to argue that one or another of our existing traditions can be refurbished to do the job. A radical Christian spirituality, based on the Sermon on the Mount — or, to be more precise, upon the now critically recovered teaching of the original Jesus, as it is presented by someone like J.D. Crossan[14] — may perhaps serve. Alternatively, a similar case might be made on behalf of a critically recovered, Westernised version of early Buddhism. The open kind of love, which in Christianity is called *agape*, in Buddhism is *metta*. That sounds hopeful, and a move of this kind, reforming and modernizing one or more of the old traditions that we have inherited, must surely be possible because the old traditions are themselves so keen to be modernized. Thus Christianity has for centuries been trying to become more world affirming, more humanitarian, and even, now, more 'Green'; and Asian Buddhism has similarly been battling to adapt itself to modern democratic politics and modern humanitarianism.

Unfortunately, this suggestion has failed in practice. The adaptation of the old traditions to the modern worldview and to modern ethics is never more than superficial and opportunistic. The deep assumptions are not changed at all, for under pressure the old cruelty and dogmatism, the old desire for 'certainties' and for the spiritual power that accrues to those who purvey them, and the old flight from time, chance, and mortality always return. The melancholy fact is that the very partial conversion of the great religions to modernity and to humanitarianism is a case of deathbed repentance and of doubtful sincerity. Recent scandals in the Roman Catholic Church, and a film like Peter Mullan's *The Magdalene Sisters* (2002), have reminded us of the horrific injustice that was common in religion until only one or two decades ago. And do not suppose that Protestantism was very much better: on the contrary, everything that was most cruel and repressive in Catholicism had a parallel in Protestantism that differed from it by only a hairsbreadth. It should be a matter for rejoicing that the general public are now being so forcibly made aware of how dark the dark side of religion was until only a few years ago.

Nor will it be easy to rescue *either* Jesus *or* the Buddha from their followers. Although they probably were, indeed, original and remarkable figures and a good deal bigger than the religions that grew around them, both of them, I say, were early and heavily overpainted and falsified. Scholarly agreement about their original teaching is in each case very hard to reach, and neither man seems likely to be able to come alive for ordinary people in his new critically-critically reconstructed form. People seem to prefer to stick to the frame in which tradition has preserved him and presented him to us.

Thus, although I still hope that something of the messages of Jesus and of the Buddha will survive, I am no longer optimistic about the possibility of reforming and renewing either 'Christianity' or 'Buddhism'. The old instinctive love of spiritual power, and the engrained hostility to this life, this world, and ordinary humanity, remain too strong ever to permit a more than token reformation. Perhaps rightly, from the traditionalist point of view, for we would-be reformers are talking about a profound reversal of the old instincts, and that cannot come easily to traditionalists. For example, instead of the traditional dogmatic faith that **holds on** to certainties guaranteed by authority, we teach an entirely different kind of faith that dispenses with any kind of anchorage or mooring, and is happy to **let go** and float freely upon sheer contingency's open sea. For the religious conservative, true faith holds on to something metaphysical, but for me true faith lets go and just floats. For the conservative, religion is aspiration after something spiritual that is beyond this world and this life; whereas for me this world and this life are outsideless and true religion is to pour oneself out into them without remainder. The conservative sees this life as a period of probation to be spent in preparing oneself for 'a good death'; but for me one should live a dying life, giving oneself into life all the time in such a way that one has no fear of death and no need to prepare for it, nor even to give it a thought. So in ways like these we are talking today about a straight reversal of all the traditional assumptions about what religion is and how it works. We want our religion to be floating, de-ethnicized, and anti-traditional. Such a reversal may be intelligible to people schooled in the Lutheran tradition, which enjoys such dialectics, but in terms of classical logic it is an obvious nonsense, and old-style religious conservatives are surely bound to reject it.

樂 樂 樂 樂 樂

Religious conservatives who want their religion to continue and to maintain its own historic identity and continuity will need to maintain in some form the traditional contrast between two distinct realms and vocabularies, the sacred and the profane. There are the common people and there are people who are **of God**; there is the world of ordinariness and there is the **better world**; there is *common humanity* and there is *the elite* (literally, the chosen). In one form and another the old distinction keeps returning, even in our relatively democratic age. But I have been suggesting that with the end of metaphysics there begins an age of outsideless or radical ordinariness. We gradually cease to associate culture with any sort of social elite: in the English language the word culture has been thoroughly democratized for about four decades now. There is no longer any **high culture**, characteristically produced for royalty and the upper classes. There is only our middle-class ordinariness — which nowadays incorporates everything that goes on in the concert hall, the art gallery, the opera house, and so on. All culture is nowadays popular. There is only one social world. In which case, surely, there is no room any longer for a separate religious vocabulary, sphere of life, set of practices and institution. Without being very explicit about it, we have abandoned belief in life after death and belief in a distinct sacred world. In a rather irregular way, religious symbolism, language, and feeling are now scattered across the world of ordinariness. Contemporary ordinariness represents, one might say, a thoroughgoing confusion, or flowing together and intermingling of the sacred and the profane, and of the (formerly) 'high' and 'low'. But this merging together of the sacred and the profane realms in the ordinariness of our own time is what the 'Abrahamic' religious traditions call the Kingdom of God on earth, and have always expected to arrive only at the end of history. In biblical terms, modern democratic politics and popular culture, together with modern super-cheap information and communications technologies, have brought to an end the old disciplinary age of the Church, and have ushered in the next epoch, the Kingdom. But in the kingdom-era there is no need and no place for any separate religious vocabulary, or institution, or professionals, or rites and other practices. In fact if I am right there is no need or place for me, or for this book. I'm redundant: I can say nothing that isn't said a great deal better in Lennon and McCartney songs, in popular cinema, in soap operas, and in jazz, or simply by the fashion industry.

So I was unwise to confess that I'd like to be the Nietzsche of religious thought, and that I'd like to write the first really truthful religious book. For if it were ever written, that book would be not the first, but the last religious book. It would end the genre. And isn't the end of religion as a distinct institution and genre already in sight today?

樂 樂 樂 樂 樂

An exception. Perhaps there is still one area in which the old sacred/profane distinction remains important. Throughout, I have been associating true religion with a special kind of open, or universal, or nonobjective joy in and love for life, for our world, and for the whole human realm. This kind of love is called in Christianity *agape*: in Mahayana Buddhism it is particularly associated with the Awakening Mind (*bodhicitta*) of the bodhisattva, who is so filled with universal love and compassion that he or she refuses any solitary salvation. The bodhisattva waits for all the others. Such a universal love is 'open', nonselective, nondiscriminating, non-fixated; and it is traditionally contrasted with erotic or profane love, which always latches fiercely onto its object, the object that awakens, attracts, and holds it — the one **with whom** one is **in love**.

For a non-realist in philosophy like me, the contrast between these two types of love is very important. Because for me there is no unseen metaphysical world out there, the religious object is not *a being*, but something as diffuse and general as (for example) **life** is. Religious love is objectless, and therefore for me has always been quite nonerotic. I have never felt in the least sexually moved while in prayer, despite what so many mystics have said. For me, loving God has always been very like what I call 'world-love' — the sort of universal benignity and warmth that moves the poet to declare that: 'God's in his heaven / All's right with the world!' Accordingly, I regard erotic excitement during prayer as the product of erotic fantasy, and as having no particular religious value. Anyone who is liable to become erotically excited during prayer — perhaps as a result of meditating upon Christ the Bridegroom and the

Spiritual Marriage — should find a lover of flesh and blood. Religious love is universal, cool, nonerotic, non-fixated, and object*less*. And *that* is what we should be cultivating when we are at prayer, or meditating.

I am suggesting that to non-realists in philosophy — to people whose outlook is postmetaphysical — the contrast between sacred and profane love is very interesting and morally important. For us God is not an objective being, and sacred love is most definitely open and objectless: it is as general as loving **It All**, or loving **Life**. It radiates benignity, and tries to exclude nobody. Profane love repeats the intense and hungry loyalty with which a child cleaves to its parent — even to a bad parent. Eros is intensely particular, exclusive, needy, jealous, and possessive. No doubt Eros needs to be schooled and moderated if it is not to become overbearing and even slightly mad, but it is part of the way we are constituted. Despite the recent rapid decline of marriage, it probably remains part of most people's lives.

Nevertheless, it is clearly true that in recent years our ideas about both profane and sacred love have been changing rapidly. Since the publication of Deleuze and Guattari's *Anti-Oedipus*[15] there has been a debate about whether the 'Oedipal' constitution of the personality need continue. Perhaps people's sexual makeup can and will change. At the same time the rise of non-realist philosophy of religion has been changing our ideas about mysticism, and about the relation between religious and sexual feeling. I have suggested that the contrast between sacred and profane love has become sharper and more important in recent years, and is now the most interesting remaining fragment of the once-great contrast between sacred and profane realms.

樂 樂 樂 樂 樂

Returning to our earlier theme, historic Christianity — and especially Latin Christianity — made a sharp distinction between the natural and supernatural orders, between Nature and Grace, the State and the Church, and the profane and sacred worlds. But this sharp contrast is not perpetual: it is maintained only during the years of grace. When Christ finally returns, it will of course disappear in his millennial kingdom on earth. And in any case — as Hegel says so well[16] — Christian theology has always tended to climax in a synthesis of the worlds. Through the Incarnation of God in Christ, and through the Pentecostal gift of the Spirit, the divine has descended to earth and diffused itself through the human realm. Christianity is the religion that is always trying to secularize itself, turning into a universal religious humanism. As we were noticing in the section before last, Christianity as an historical institution, movement, and task always seeks to fulfil its mission and go beyond itself. It seeks self-cancellation, self-transcendence. It wants to make itself redundant; it longs to become historically obsolete.

Now, at last, that ancient hope is fulfilled. The Church is indeed finished. It should be delighted, because this was what it always longed for. But it is not pleased, not a bit pleased.

樂 樂 樂 樂 樂

I am hearing objections to my idea of universal, objectless, non-fixated love, for life, for the world and for one's fellow-human. This notion of a loving disposition that just *radiates* universally, without definitely attaching itself to anything in particular, attracts a double hostility. It is said to be too abstract and philosophical, reflecting the old platonic belief that the universal is always nobler and higher in value than any mere particular can hope to be. And secondly, it is what D.H. Lawrence scornfully calls 'white love', too bloodless for biological organisms like us. Our proper love is sexual: it is driven by hormones and by life's striving to extend and propagate itself. As for white love, it's chilly, it's an affair of the will, and nobody really desires to be its object. It's **as cold as charity**.

I appreciate this criticism, and perhaps should have done more to forestall it. In Buddhism *metta* is always explained by analogy with the mother's love for her child, which is not jealous or exclusive in the manner of erotic love, but on the contrary can always add another one when another one comes along. This is a biological, not a philosophical, analogy. I try to make a similar move when I try to base my notion of objectless universal love upon simple animal pleasure in life, in being alive and in ebullient high spirits. Like mother-love, high spirits can always welcome another one into the throng. To that I would add pleasure in our continually changing sense experience just as such, and pleasure in the running of language in our heads. I have often tried to emphasize the need to educate the senses — especially those of sight and hearing —to enrich people's pleasure in life. Modern education is highly deficient in this respect, but I was lucky as a schoolboy to come under the influence of the art teacher Ian Fleming-Williams. As for the move from particular to universal, I would wish to follow Nietzsche and the Paris-school painters in making it via *the dance*. Dancing is highly social and is good at helping us to get out of enclosed individual self-consciousness and into being solar. Being (inevitably) somewhat inclined to moroseness and introversion, I have always admired the sort of sociable, high-spirited, solar person of whom it is said that she is **the life and soul of the party**. So when I talk about non-fixated, objectless, universal love, I am not talking about something abstract, bodiless, and emotion-free. Rather, I am talking about an exhilarated, selfless enjoyment of, delight in and gratitude for just the flow of daily experience, the movement of life itself, and the endless self-renewing variety of the human world.

It is a mark of the religious character of this joy in life that it can be, and quite often is, joy in affliction: it can be experienced strongly and can be sustaining, even in the hardest times. The peoples who inhabit the harshest environments are often found to love life as much as anyone.

樂 樂 樂 樂 樂

If true religion is the love of life, joy in life, and solar living, how are we to find the right vocabulary for articulating and celebrating it and training ourselves to live it effectively? Human beings have, it seems, always wanted to believe that there is such a thing as the *right* vocabulary, in which all the gods and spirits are known by their real names, and all religious truth is definitely expressed. Indeed, they have usually supposed that in their own religion they have already been given the right vocabulary and the whole truth.

Today, it is obvious that all such ideas are absurd. It is absurd to suppose that the name by which we call God is God's *real* name, the Name by which he's told us he wants to be known henceforth. It is absurd to suppose that our language — be it Hebrew, Arabic, Sanskrit, or whatever — was used by the gods in the heavenly world before we ever existed. It is absurd to suppose that the written text of the scriptures was composed by God in the eternal world and then subsequently dictated by an angel to Moses or Muhammad. Indeed, such ideas scarcely need refutation: we need only to state them clearly to see that they are pre-Enlightenment notions that cannot be taken seriously today. For us, now

1. There is no specially-privileged right vocabulary.
2. There is no divinely approved right 'angle', or order of exposition.
3. There is no One, True, and Final system of religious doctrine, God's own story about himself, told just as he wants it to be told.
4. Religious teaching in the future cannot be framed as merely a simplified and liberalized version of the scripture-and-doctrine-based religion we have known hitherto. On the contrary, religious teaching must not again ever be allowed to become codified, fixed, and sacrosanct. On the contrary, it must have the all-round corrigibility that is the mark of every modern system of knowledge.
5. In religion, ethics, and the philosophy of life the price of truth from now on is constant self-criticism and the readiness to remint all one's metaphors.

6. It follows from all this that secondhand belief in creeds drawn up by other people in the past, and handed down to us, is now of no religious value whatever. The only religious beliefs that avail are ones that we have framed ourselves, or found in ourselves, and have checked out in life and in conversation with others.

7. The religion of the future, then, will be a pilgrim religion that we ourselves are consciously making and remaking all the time. We will be like artists, permanent pilgrims with no fixed abode, improvising our own spiritualities and our own life-stories as we go along. Indeed, this is how most of us already are.

樂 樂 樂 樂 樂

The main threads of my argument are now in place. I have maintained that the religion of the future will be a religion of joy in and love for life — *this* life, ordinary human life. This new outlook is already established amongst us, as is shown by the remarkable number of new and quasi-religious sayings about life that have come into ordinary language during the past half century or so. Just about everything that used to be said about God has now been rephrased and refocused to become a saying about life.

The new religion is a religion of immediate ethical commitment to life, to the human world, and to the neighbour, just in the here and now. When we can pour ourselves out so completely into our own living that we become 'solar', we may be said to be living a dying life, and thereby to have conquered death. We are easy, going: happy to be passing or transient. But for historical reasons this is not easy for us, and the question arises of what vocabulary, what rituals, and what theology we will need in order to train ourselves to become habitually solar.

The turn to everyday life and to ordinariness may be seen as a long-term consequence of the Protestant Reformation, when Martin Luther and his Katharine left their religious Orders and established a family home. But it was also a consequence of the scientific revolution, for the revolution in cosmology brought about by Copernicus and Galileo ended the traditional contrast between two different worlds, the heavenly world above and the earthly world here below — two worlds that were formerly thought to be made of quite different materials and subject to quite different laws. This contrast between earth and heaven was basic, not only to cosmology but to all religion. It underlay all forms of the idea that religion is a distinct and higher sphere of life with its own institutions, its own vocabulary, and its own laws, making a uniquely authoritative claim upon us and promising us a blessed destiny beyond this world. But as a result of Galileo's work this division of reality into two great worlds has come to an end. The universe, and life, and language now comprise a single, great, unbounded continuum. There is only one world, and it is *our* world, *this* world, the *human* world, the world of our *language*. Our language runs everywhere with equal ease, covering everything, forming everything, and making everything 'bright'. There is no longer, in the old way, a visibly distinct and privileged sacred world above, of which we all stand in awe, and which has its own distinctive vocabulary and laws. We simply cannot pretend nowadays to maintain the old clear contrast between sacred history and profane history, or between the sacred scriptures and the humanities (*litterae sacrae, litterae humaniores*). It is all one to us now.

It follows that we cannot expect the religion of ordinary everyday life to imitate the older religions and to develop its own distinctive worldview, institutions, vocabulary, and ways of thinking. Nowadays the only sacred thing left is ordinariness itself.

In the Bronze Age some of the first cities were built beside great rivers that flooded once a year. In these cities, in places like Egypt and Mesopotamia, temples were founded on the very spot where, it was claimed, the waters of the primal Flood had receded and dry land had first appeared. On the primal mound the creator-god had sat as he made the world and set everything in order. Through his image, he was now enthroned permanently in the Temple on the same spot. Each year, creation was ritually renewed and the world was set in order again.

Today all knowledge — and indeed everything — is constructed within human language, by human beings. The primal mound, the place of creation, the spot from which organizing power radiates over the entire world is our human ordinariness. All our more specialized vocabularies and knowledge systems go back to and are rooted in ordinary language. Our ordinary language is old and highly idiomatic; it is so compressed, so irregular and so complex that we do not understand it clearly. But as the religion and worldview of the future become at last completely this-worldly, humanistic, and given over to the present moment, the language through which it all first expresses itself and in which it is most fully at home becomes, simply, ordinary language.

This at last explains why I have been finding the evidence of an emergent new religious consciousness within the changes that are currently taking place just in ordinary language. The striking new idioms, and the most pungent new metaphors, that first caught my eye a few years ago are simply the new religious insights that are being democratized in our own time.

An interesting corollary of all this is that the new religion of life has no creed, no technical theology of its own, and does not need any door-to-door evangelists to spread it. It is self-spreading. All the work is done within and by ordinary language, because ordinary language is itself now the only sacred language we have. All the new religious feelings, insights, and ideas quickly become coded into ordinary language in the form of attractive and arresting new idioms and metaphors, which spread and become common property with extraordinary rapidity.

It follows from this that the present book is also redundant. Perhaps it is a work of anti-theology, explaining why theology as traditionally understood has now worked itself out of a job and made itself redundant. Perhaps, indeed, my three little *Everyday Speech* books were disregarded because, as they themselves say, everyone already knows and accepts everything they contain. Which means that they are not needed. Are they?

樂 樂 樂 樂 樂

If ordinariness, the ordinariness of everyday human life, is now the religious object, and if religion is currently giving up any appeal to or yearning after anything outside present ordinariness, then surely we can expect to find that ordinary people and ordinary language no longer bother to have any views either way about life after death. Haven't I been saying that ordinariness is quite unspeculative? Surely we may expect to find that lively and vigorous young people who live at or close to the centre of life are so absorbed in life that they never give death a thought: and have I not been saying that they are quite right? There is no need for them to give death a thought. Death isn't anything. There's nothing there to think. The only sensible way to prepare for death is to **live life to the full**, *really* the full. Just by so living one is doing all there is to do about death. One is **making the most of the time one has left**.

Sometimes you may think that the new religion of life is 'Kingdom' religion, and that as such it is the long-awaited fulfilment of the whole history of religion hitherto. At other times you may think that the new religion of life is no more than mere Epicureanism: **Let us eat, drink, and be merry; for tomorrow we die**. Either way, it is unspeculative and undoctrinal: the religion of life does not really need any doctrine-system or any creed. The only doctrines it needs are doctrines asserting the irrelevance or falsity of various doctrines left over from the past that still exercise some lingering influence amongst us.

Yet in practice you are sometimes troubled, I am sometimes troubled, and ordinary people are sometimes evasive and ambiguous, about life after death. The reason for this is that in the old Augustinian-Christian doctrine-system human beings were originally created by God to be naturally immortal here on earth. It could therefore be presumed that in the far future, when human beings would be redeemed and the original inno-cence of Paradise would be restored on earth, we would regain our origi-nal natural immortality. In the future Age of Gold, people would live forever on this earth. So it was believed, in many religious traditions.

As it has turned out, though, we have done well, but we have not done quite *that* well. We have greatly increased the average human life span, so that in the developed countries the average expectation of life at birth for both sexes is now greater than the biblical allotted span. That's good going: but we do still die, and for up to a third of us the last year or two are pretty undignified. So my solar conquest of death is by no means as complete as the old theological conquest of death claimed to be. My message is that if we can learn to love life sufficiently intensely, and if we can learn to give ourselves to life all the time with sufficiently 'female' physical generosity, then we will find that dying is as easy as falling asleep. We'll be able to sail right into death, loving life and giving ourselves to it all the way. But we do still die. We are transient, and in my account there is no eternal Reality or eternal world.

So you may be forgiven for thinking that on my account death is still a problem, and for wondering what ordinary language really says about it now.

In ordinary language there is a wide range of phrases and metaphori-cal expressions using the word **dead**. The contrast between the living and the dead is a contrast between what is active, moving, and playing its part in the exchanges of life, and what is inert, extinguished, cold, dark, and no longer operative. There is of course an interesting and attractive set of idioms that use **dead** to mean accurate, exact, certain, or absolute: they include, for example, **dead reckoning**, **dead shot**, **dead ringer**, and **dead certain**. Otherwise, the vast majority of idioms simply use **dead** to mean no longer functioning effectively at all, as when a fire is **dead**, a law is a **dead letter**, a ship is **dead in the water**, or a language is **dead**.

What then is the status of a corpse? Historically there was no prop-erty in corpses, and it was rather unusual for the family to put up a strong claim for the corpse. It was often spoken of as **the remains** of the person, or **all that was mortal** of the person, idioms implying the belief that the real person was something immortal which had now departed. A trace of the old belief in life after death remains yet in talk of dying as **passing on** or **passing away**. Otherwise there has been a remarkable change during the past half century. The family members now claim possession of the corpse, the *entire* corpse, with great determination, and they speak of the corpse as the real person. This was all very obvious in the scandal some years ago over the retention by pathology departments of organs from the bodies of children who had died in hospital, and in the response of relatives to the great terrorist attacks of 2000/2001 in the eastern United States and at Bali, Indonesia. People insist on having the dead person, whole, in their possession so that she can be fixed in some place of commemoration where they can visit her and (perhaps) speak to her. Linked with this is the idea that the dead are somehow **up there, looking down upon us** — very like the photographs of one's dead kinfolk that line the walls of a Chinese clan shrine. In our society we do not have anything quite like a clan shrine, but each of us has an inner shrine in his own memory, where our dead look benevolently down upon us and remain forever exactly **as they were in life**. They do not change, because we no longer suppose the dead to be living in another world. We think of them as being now located in cemeteries, and in our memories. In both places they are still present, as they were and quite unchanged. We cherish their memory, we are aware of their continuing influence, and in a poetical way we may speak to them. But they are of course dead and not alive. So much for the status of the dead in our culture.

One more point is to be added: elsewhere I have recently begun to make a clear and sharp distinction between **my life** and life in general.[17] **My life** is my personal span. It is the life of which I am the subject. In recent years people have begun determinedly to claim full ownership of their own lives and the sole right to determine the course of their own lives. **My life**, of course, is finite: if it were not so, it would be too big an object for me to be able realistically to claim the right to shape it, determine its course, and accept responsibility for it as a whole. So **my life** is finite: it is my own project, my soul, whereas life in general, the larger human scene, goes on indefinitely. The distinction here seems to have become clear and important in modern ordinary language, especially in association with modern feminism and women's struggle for the right to choose their own path in life. Rising prosperity and better social administration have made it possible to envisage and to plan, and to claim rights over the course of one's life as a whole, for the first time.

At this point a new argument enters philosophy. I see for the first time that it is a great good fully to own my life, confessing that it is all mine and that I must accept full responsibility for it. But I can only own my life in this way if it is finite. So I see that I must accept death and finitude as necessary conditions for my being the person I know I must try to be, namely someone whose life is his own.

These considerations were introduced by the young Heidegger. But I want to add to them. For we are constituted as persons not only by own-ing our own lives, but also by the loves we own.[18] But they too are finite and have the effect of committing us to mortality.

樂 樂 樂 樂 樂

At one stage in the 1980s, I seemed to myself to be able to think sys-tematically. My head was clear, words ran freely, and ideas seemed to spread out before me already interconnected and organized into patterns. It seemed as easy as unrolling a carpet by pushing it away, and watching the design emerge. All I had to do was get it all down on paper.

This impression of clarity and the confidence it gave me was mis-taken, because in the same period I often subsequently found my ideas very hard to understand, and even harder to explain to others. Within a year or two doctrines which at their birth had been so glowingly clear to me were becoming obscure and difficult.

That, I think, is why in more recent years my method has changed and I now, as Arthur Dewey has put it, 'think in riffs'.[19] I state a theme in a simple and preliminary way, play with it, turn it around, try a few varia-tions on it, stretch it a bit — and so continue until I feel ready to restate it, in amplified form. The same process then begins again: again I try to find new angles, new objections, and new developments, and slowly build up the argument. The idea is that for both the author and the reader this gradual elaboration eventually produces a stronger and clearer outcome. Under the old regime my books tended to be dismissed and forgotten long before they had ever been understood: now I can reasonably hope that at any rate a handful of people might stay with me and understand me, because they will have been with me as I have tried to **think through** my ideas. And indeed, you have been with me thus far in our present enquiry.

Our theme is the theory of religion — and I am not talking here about a scholars' theory of what religion in all its enormous historical and geographical range and variety has been. I am not talking about a large-scale general theory that might do for *religions-geschichte*, or 'the compara-tive study of religions', the sort of job that evolutionary theory has done for biology. Nor am I producing a theory like that presented in *After God*. No, I'm talking about a theory of religion that might be personally helpful to people like you and me — modern Westerners who are temperamen-tally highly religious, and who want there to *be* religion, but who know that virtually all received religious ideas, doctrines, and institutions are obsolete. In short, I am here looking not for a large-scale, empirically based general theory or explanation of religion, but merely for a way of looking at religion that can help highly-secularized people like us to see how it might become a live option for us again.

The formula I begin from is this: religion is cosmic emotion. I am often accused of being a dry rationalist who underestimates the importance of the emotions, but in fact my thinking has been moving in the opposite direction — towards emotivism — for many years. We are animals: our life largely consists in, or rides upon, a continuous outpouring stream of biological feeling. This turbid river of emotion, the basis of one's personal life, was traditionally referred to by philosophers as 'the passions'. It varies from one person to another in ways that used to be described in terms of each person's typical **balance of humours** or **temperament**. Today, we may speak of a person's **disposition** or **mood**; but the truth is probably that we never had, and still do not have, any very satisfactory vocabulary in this area.

As well as the standing, endogenously-generated stream of emotion — or typical mix of emotions — upon which personal life rides, there is also our constantly changing emotional response to incoming stimuli from the environment. Both cognition and evaluation grow out of this primal feeling-response to the events of life.

Finally, there is a third major factor in our emotional life. We are intensely social beings, and the emotions are highly contagious. Feeling that is shared with others becomes more definite, is greatly enhanced, and gives us greater pleasure. That is why we usually arrange to have a companion when we go to a concert, an exhibition, a cinema, or a new place. Sharing it helps to fix the experience and make it more identifiable.

In this first brief sketch, then, each person's flowing emotional life has three tributaries: there is my temperament or disposition, the typical mix of endogenously-generated outflowing feeling that supports my personal life all the time; there is my ever-changing emotional response to input from the environment; and there is the social communing with others through which feeling-life gains clarification, enhancement, and pleasure — as when we **feel better** after a good **heart-to-heart**, or when we remember who was with us when we first saw this or that.

Next we turn to the relation between feeling and language — which is, of course, the chief means by which we publicize feeling, sharing it and giving it meaning. As in Schopenhauer's philosophy the incoherent uncomfortable striving of 'the Will' seeks relief by coming out all the time into symbolic representation, so our outpouring life of feeling seeks expression. This means that it seeks symbolic expression — perhaps in music or in dance, but above all in words. When we have been able to get our feelings **off our chests** and into the right words they are relieved indeed, but by no means *only* relieved, for by getting out into concrete symbolic expression our feeling becomes more definite, more enhanced, more pleasurable, and more generally available to others — that is, more public. Even more yet, in our fullest and most adequate self-expression we find that we **become ourselves** and are able **to recognize ourselves**. And there is more to tell; for it is our differential feeling-response to our experience that puts both the *colour* and the *contrast* into our entire vision of the world.

From this we glimpse a little of the extraordinary power of language. Language's power to **make something** out of our feelings —to make poetry, to make the world, to make ourselves — is so great that we should probably also think of language as actively eliciting the emotions that it wants to express. To put the point afresh, one may say that form often seems to precede matter: our language actually draws out the feeling-life that it is supported by and that it expresses. Following in the Schopenhauer-Freud tradition we are apt to think of the emotions as powerful natural forces that build up a great head of steam inside us. These natural drives seek natural expression — in sex or in violence, for example — but if social prohibitions block their natural expressions, they may seek to evade the censorship and find some permitted symbolic outlets instead. The model here is very nineteenth century: it pictures Nature as coming first, and Culture as battling with rather mixed success to hold down Nature, which nevertheless often slips out in disguise. But I am suggesting that the image of the self as a steam engine, with the emotions as being like steam under great pressure inside us and art as a safety valve, is misleading. On the contrary, I am suggesting so great is the power of language (and of art, and of religion) that very often we should see language as itself awakening our emotions, drawing them out and giving them the courage, as well as the means to emerge into public expression.

This reverses the traditional relationship between Nature and Culture. In nineteenth-century thinking, from Schopenhauer to Freud, Nature came first. It was an unruly collection of powerful desires and drives, each interested only in its own gratification. Culture battled to discipline and regulate Nature, laying down the law about the conditions under which it could be permitted either natural or substitute gratifications. Typically, the biological drive (which is a bit of Nature) comes up against the barrier of Culture's censorship, and manages to sneak past in disguised symbolic form as the symptom. Typical symptoms might include giveaway body language, scraps of religious ritual, works of art, and the contents of dreams. The common factor is that in all this Schopenhauer-to-Freud thinking, Nature comes before Culture, and Mr Hyde precedes Dr Jekyll. But after Jacques Lacan there begins an attempt to reverse the order and give the priority to the cultural form. Language begins to be seen as producing reality — i.e., as evoking or eliciting or calling forth the feelings to which it gives expression.

The postmodernist attempt systematically to put Culture first, and give it priority over Nature, is often seen as extremist and paradoxical. Yet in a sense it is obvious. For example, we teach the young a sense of humour by telling them lots of jokes and mocking them if they fail to understand them. And again, we teach shy young persons how to fall in love by giving them stacks of romantic novels to read. In religion, similarly, we teach people faith by introducing them to religious practice, as when we say that the only way to acquire belief in God and get it right is by the practice of prayer, praying as if one believes until one has learnt belief. So in cases such as these we get to the supposedly natural aptitude or feeling (a sense of humour, falling in love, the desire for God) not directly, but via the elaborated cultural expression that is usually pictured as being late and secondary. That is the only way we can proceed, and therefore it is the way we always do proceed. To make the point yet again, to find out whether my child has a 'natural' ear for music, I must send her to piano lessons, which are highly 'cultural': how else could we proceed?

Language, then, has great power over our life of natural feeling. It draws it out, differentiates it, forms it, channels it, and gives it expression. All of which helps us to understand why it is that the feeling-life of human beings is so much more intense, richer and sometimes more excessive than the feeling-life of animals. We are very stormy: compared with us, most animals are relatively sober, rational creatures who do not waste their energies. Indeed, they cannot afford to waste energy: the exigencies of survival require them to be quietly efficient. Thus the feeling-life of animals is usually kept closely in line with their immediate biological needs.

And us? We have language, and with it we have an astounding hypertrophy of culture. Because language is so easily bent back upon itself, it quickly introduces us to irony, humour, reflexivity, a sense of doubleness, and consciousness. It therefore breaks free of the biological demands of the present moment, and so greatly enhances our feeling-life that it makes us capable of cosmic emotion. By this I mean that language introduces us to a feeling-life far beyond anything animals can experience. Language gets us trying to think outside ourselves and to feel beyond ourselves. We feel *awe* at the greatness of the world, awe and dread at the human condition, fear as we contemplate the unknown future and our own deaths, and cosmic love for natural beauty and for our own feeling of being alive.

This discussion enables us to recognize a dialectical relationship between language and religious feeling. First, religious language (and symbolism and ritual . . .) tends to teach cosmic emotion by evoking it and making it habitual to us who are from childhood trained in religion. This is particularly true, both for good and ill, of symbolically rich forms of religion such as Roman Catholicism, and many a lapsed Catholic has testified that whatever has happened to her personal beliefs, the old symbols will continue to evoke the old emotions until the end of her life. Even a lapsed Catholic remains indelibly a Catholic.

Second, I have also suggested that in an older and more primal sense it was language itself that first made us religious. Because words are general, any use of language may evoke other places and occasions than the present, and therefore language tends to prise us free from the animal's customary state of total absorption in its own present biological imperatives. Language, as ordinary people say, **makes you think**; and I have suggested that because language is so easily used to refer to itself, it everywhere teaches people a certain doubleness, which is manifest in irony, humour, reflexivity (banter), consciousness, and self-consciousness. But when language breaks free in this way, and we become self-mocking, self-aware, self-conscious, and (in short) *spirit* — then emotion too breaks free, and becomes boundless, cosmic, sublime. One becomes a single, self-questioning individual, filled with wonder, awe, dread, and even fear and horror at the mystery of one's own human existence.

We have been playing with the formula, *religion is cosmic emotion*. Now, we can try to be more specific about cosmic emotion.

A number of writers have suggested that there is one particular religious emotion, such as the sense of awe and dread that one feels in the presence of the Holy, the Sacred, or the numinous. The numinous is *mysterium tremendum et fascinans*, awesome and riveting: it fills us with dread, but **we can't take our eyes off it**.

A rather different candidate for the role of being the specifically and distinctively religious experience is the extravertive type of mystical experience, in which objects in the external world are seen as if one is Vincent van Gogh and about to have an epileptic fit. The object is throbbing, highly coloured, and super-real. There is a strong feeling of significance, or 'meaningfulness' — whatever that is.

I reject both these accounts, and agree with William James when he declares that 'there is no one elementary religious emotion'. But I disagree with James when he adds that there is only 'a common storehouse of emotions upon which religious objects may draw', and then goes on to say that religious love, for example, is 'only man's natural emotion of love directed to a religious object'.[20] That is mistaken, because it fails sufficiently to stress that the religious 'object' is not an object like ordinary finite objects, and therefore religious love is not at all like ordinary profane love.

Let us pursue once again this particular example of profane and sacred love. Profane love, *Eros*, is closely related to our biological makeup. It is awakened by, and it fastens upon, a particular finite object to which it cleaves with intense, jealous, and exclusive attachment. It is very 'realistic', in the sense that it is *allocentric*: it starts from the other person, and its whole attention is filled with the objective reality of the other. For me, it has to be this one particular person, and no other.

The divine love or universal compassion of which religion speaks (*agape, metta*) is quite different. It has no finite object; indeed, it is not based in its object at all. It is an objectless, indiscriminating, and boundlessly generous love. It flows out, in all directions. It does not 'respect persons' as the old phrase had it, but is like the sun which rises on the evil and the good alike, and the rain which falls both on the just and on the unjust.[21] Agapeistic love is cosmic emotion, a boundless love of life, love of **It All**, love of **Everything**. To love in this way is to love God, because this sort of love just *is* God. It is a universal disposition that overflows the biological limits by which other and lesser loves are confined. When we understand what this love is, we recognize what a profound error is made by all those people and institutions that believe in realistic theism. The realist God is not God at all, and object-fixated or allocentric love is not divine love. The official church has got God very badly wrong.

Against this background we can now define what were traditionally called 'the religious affections'. They are all those emotions that can become cosmic, i.e., infinitised or boundless. When I am thankful to God, for example, I am cosmically grateful, **grateful for Everything**, grateful to **It All** and for **It All, grateful to life**. I am, for the moment, utterly content that all things are as they are, and I do not want anything to be any different. I feel blessed, privileged, just glad to be alive. That's cosmic thanksgiving or gratitude, and again what makes it divine is its objectlessness, for I am not grateful *to* anybody, but am just boundlessly grateful.

Years ago, my companion and I scrambled to a Lake District peak — Red Screes, in fact — and sat down to draw breath and gaze at the view. Near us was a small party of very ordinary north-country folk who were awed by the beauty of the day. 'I feel privileged' murmured one middle-aged woman — one of the purest and simplest religious confessions I have ever heard. Few of us ever say anything better than that. Indeed, I'm not sure that there's anything better than that to be said, ever. That's my theory of religion in a nutshell: true religion is to be able quite unaffectedly to say something like that, on an occasion like that, and mean it. (And I should remark that a fellow human being — for example, one who is in trouble — may well prompt cosmic emotion. It is so easy to quote a landscape example that one may neglect to mention other and very different examples.)

樂 樂 樂 樂 樂

If you are a religious person, you will have noticed that genuine religious feeling seems to have many of the traditional attributes of God. It is not in any way volatile, but it is constant. It is not attached to, nor dependent upon, any particular object, but it is free. It arises from itself — *a se*, in Latin — and *aseity* was one of the traditional attributes of God. It is not passionate or turbulent, but full and deep. It seems to embrace the whole world, unbounded — infinite — and indiscriminate. It pours out of the self, and in that way is rather like the feeling for the sublime, especially in landscape, which is why when I want to evoke it I tend to think at once of the landscapes of my heart in Northern England.

When we experience strong religious feeling we understand what it once was to believe in God. God was like this. Perhaps when I go walking in my favourite landscapes today I am unconsciously seeking to recover the intense theistic religious feeling I had at the age of twenty or so. But in a more rational moment I recognize that pure and intense religious feeling really is *a se*, of itself. It does not depend upon the existence of a metaphysical God, and in our entirely post-metaphysical age it is important that I should testify that it can and does still survive in us as strong and deep as ever. Indeed, religious experience after God is in some ways purer and better than it was in the epoch of belief in God. In recent writings I have called it *world-love* and *the love of life*.

Ludwig Feuerbach deserves great credit for having been almost the first to have understood these things.[22] He salvages the divine attributes for us after the death of God: he transfers the divine attributes to, for example, love, so that we can continue to experience them and be blessed by them. Poor man, he has few sympathetic readers who appreciate the religious value of his work.

樂 樂 樂 樂 樂

As a standard topic in the philosophy of religion, 'the Problem of Evil' owes much to the great philosopher G.W. Leibniz.[23] It was he in particular who established the use of the phrase 'metaphysical evil' to describe the permanent and irremovable limits by which the whole created Universe and everything in it is beset. God is necessarily unique, and the Universe, not being God, has to be less than God — not infinite, but merely finite; not necessary but contingent and not eternal but merely temporal. The metaphysical 'evils' (really, just imperfections) are therefore contingency, temporality, and finitude — or in common speech, Chance, Time, and Death. After Kant, as Western philosophy gradually abandons the idea that there is any unseen Eternal Order of Reason beyond the changing world here below, the traditional metaphysical evils become central to philosophy, and the theory of religion here being put forward accordingly starts from them. For example, I often suggest that instead of seeing life's metaphysical limits as 'imperfections' or evils, we should perhaps revalue them drastically.

Contingency, temporality, and finitude beset, not just the world and everything in it, but — and notably — language itself. The linguistic sign is always 'arbitrary' or contingent, and every linguistic utterance delivers its own meaning — never quite complete and unambiguous — only as it completes its own passing away.

In the theory I am proposing, it is our acquisition of language that distances us a little from the old animal immersion in our own biology and its immediate demands, and awakens us to the inescapability of metaphysical evil. Language makes us much more aware, not only of other times and places, but also of other persons and therefore of other points of view than our own. And, I have been arguing, language hugely amplifies our emotions. The primates, generally, are relatively highly sociable and therefore excitable, but we humans are stormier yet. Making us aware of the future, language gives us intense *fear*, for example: fear of impending disaster and fear of death such as animals can never know until the moment when they take their last steps into the *abattoir*.

Pascal's *Pensées*[24] gives to Europeans their classic (and still their favourite) account of the emotions that fill us as we contemplate the human condition and the puzzling beauty of the world about us. We are filled in varying degrees with frustration and bafflement, awe and wonder, love and gratitude, horror, dread, and sheer terror. These cosmic feelings can be quite overwhelmingly vast and impossible to escape from. They are uncomfortable, for they make us self-conscious: I myself am made to feel small and contemptible by the very scale and violence of my own feeling. What am I to do to gain relief from all this?

The job of religion is (roughly) to present us with great reconciling symbols and rituals that help to resolve our turbulent, conflicting feelings. If the symbol is big and powerful enough to embrace and incorporate our conflicting feelings — and especially, our negative feelings — in full, then it converts them into the properly religious type of feeling. Anxious self-concern entirely disappears: one's consciousness expands and becomes 'divine' — that is, motionless, peaceful, glittering, blessed, silently outpouring, and absorbed.

Religion's job then is to resolve painful, conflicting, excessive feeling and to turn it into the blessed 'religious' sort of feeling. Religious symbols, words, rituals are the tools that do the job. Let us take as an example the question of life, transience, and death. We know only too well that we will die, and we also know that whatever symbols religion offers to help us to cope with our own mortality must not deny death, or they will not work. The symbols won't be plausible. So the religious symbol must achieve some kind of synthesis of life and death, while doing full justice to the reality of both.

At this point many or most cultures make a move that copes with our dread of death and of the corpse by dividing the dead person into two parts. There is a fearsome part that needs to be firmly removed from society and disposed of in such a way that everyone can feel quite confident that it will not come back and trouble us; and there is another part that is to be equally-firmly enthroned or established in the sacred world, in our corporate memory, and in the public record — and this is the *real* dead person, the one we love and will never forget, whom we will always speak of as being **up there and looking** benevolently **down upon us**. Thus the body-soul distinction helped people in many traditional societies to cope with their ambivalent feelings in the presence of death: feelings of horror at the sight of the corpse and feelings of extreme grief at the sudden, final loss of the dead person. Funerary rites sealed up the corpse in a place firmly out of sight, while simultaneously enthroning the dead person's spirit in the corporate memory. That done, everyone was happy, and normal life could be resumed.[25] And it is true that many of us find that our dead are more vividly and continually present to us now than they were when they were still alive.

Even today, in the modern West, this remains a pretty satisfactory account of the way we deal publicly with the death of *other people*; but it keeps very quiet about the question of whether anything of subjective consciousness survives, and it does not do anything to help me cope with my present knowledge of my own mortality. What do we make of the sense of shock we'll feel when we are told — as many of our friends have already been told — that we have about six months, or one year or two, left? What do we do, what do we feel, as simple extinction looms? For make no mistake: we all of us know in our hearts that that's what awaits us.

We also know that the standard consolations don't work. The official answer, that we will live on in other people's memories, in our genetic descendants, and in various sorts of public record, is no consolation. The official philosophical answers given by a string of writers from Lucretius' *de Rerum Natura* to the young Wittgenstein's *Tractatus Logico-Philosophicus* say roughly that 'death is not lived-through', or 'since you'll never know you're dead, there's nothing to fear. In fact, death is nothing: you never reach it. Death is a boundary, but we never actually cross it. And since death is nothing, we shouldn't bother with it, but instead should think only of life.' But, emotionally speaking, that's no consolation either. There's all the difference in the world between the wonderful and seemingly infinite openness of life for a young person who **has it all before her**, and the desperate narrowness of the prospect before an old person for whom everything has closed in, and there's **nothing left to look forward to**. The very old person **has no hope**: what are we to say about *that*?

Here religion works on the imagination and the emotions, by first presenting us with powerful images that show us in full what Death is, and what Life is, and then offering us as the religious goal a state that is a kind of synthesis of the two great principles. It is often called eternal life, and is associated with God and the heavenly world. God is very much a *living* God, whilst at the same time being in many ways rather like a dead person. For example, he is enthroned in the same exalted place inside our heads — **up there**, ordinary language calls it. There God and our dead sit together, **looking down upon us** benignly. Thus popular tradition tries to comfort the dying with slogans like *mors janua vitae*, death is the gateway to a new and better life; and until not very long ago it seemed to work well enough. But nowadays the way dying people talk to me about death indicates only too clearly, and too often, that it doesn't work anymore. It is not quite convincing, either emotionally or cosmologically.

A method of synthesizing Life and Death that really does work will have to be phrased in terms of this world only, because there is no other, and it will have to be intensely and purely emotive, because it is no good whatever unless it cures us completely of the primitive horror and dread that fill us when we are confronted by the passage of time and the close approach of our own death. It will also have to be something that we begin to practise now, for suppose that in a few years' time the doctors suddenly inform you of the results of tests that show you do have a terminal illness. How will you react? Calmly, in the confidence that our life is outsideless and that you will, of course, have no problem in going on loving life and saying Yes to life until your last breath? Or will you react as if to a heavy blow, followed by something like a panic attack? The answer is that we can only be fully confident of being able to cope with our own mortality if we start living 'after death' *now*.

This way of living that synthesizes Life and Death is called *solar living*, the metaphor depending upon the well-known fact that the process by which the sun lives is the very same process by which it is also always dying. The same might be said of a lit candle. We should see Life and Death, not as two distinct and opposite conditions, one of which is followed by the other, but as two sides of a single sheet of paper. I am my own life and I am my own mortality, indissolubly. To learn this emotionally, we should practise living by giving ourselves into life, by giving ourselves away all the time, by surrendering ourselves into our own transience. We should reject at once the myriad devices by which people try to arrest, or conceal, or forget the passage of time. By the practice of solar living we can transmute all our violent, conflicting feelings about life and time and death into pure religious feeling. That is eternal life in the present moment. If we really try to practise solar living, then we have conquered death and will have no reason for anxiety as we await the results of those hospital tests.

樂 樂 樂 樂 樂

To complete the present short statement of our theory of religion, I need to explain why I have come to see the study of ordinary language as being a hitherto neglected, but now vital, method of religious enquiry. The answer, briefly, is this: in the last hundred years or so we have gradually come to see the world of ordinary human life as being, quite simply, the only world there is. Previously, for thousands of years, human beings had generally believed that this world is only 'appearance'. Behind it or beyond it there is a greater invisible world, variously pictured as the supernatural world of religion, or philosophy's 'intelligible' world of eternal truths and values. People habitually saw our own apparent or visible world as being founded in, sustained and governed by, and eventually returning into the eternal world above.

Laying down his own version of these ideas, Plato wonders how our language, which we ordinarily use to describe things and manage our lives in the world below, can also be used to speak about things in the eternal or supernatural world above. He recognises the obvious difficulty: we have to take words that ordinarily refer to our sense-experience of fleeting particular things and learn to use them instead to refer to timeless truths, values, and 'forms'. That is about as far as Plato takes the matter, and it is enough to indicate why we have inherited a picture of philosophy and of theology as élite, otherworldly subjects for which students must learn a special technical vocabulary and ways of thinking. The wisest and best human being was long considered to be the monk, who was a sort of spiritual stargazer and spent his life in the contemplation of eternal verities. Hence a puzzling feature of the surviving writings of the Middle Ages: they have left us a huge quantity of philosophical and theological literature about the ideal world above, but far too little information about how they regarded and managed more mundane affairs.

In the later Middle Ages, however, there began a very gradual turn to this world which involved a large-scale revaluation of secular life and culture, and eventually the development of a whole range of secular 'subjects' — branches of knowledge. The process has been very slow and long drawn-out, and it has taken many centuries of debate before people in general have felt able to accept purely immanent (i.e. this-worldly and only-human) accounts of knowledge, of moral values, of human psychology, of language, and so on. It was difficult to give up the old habit of validating everything by anchoring it in the eternal world. But broadly speaking, by the end of the nineteenth century one could begin to envisage 'the end of Platonism' — the end of all forms of the belief that this world (including our values, our intellectual standards, and all our pictures of the way things go) is governed from, and upheld by, and oriented towards a point outside it. People could begin to be able to say that our world, this world, has no outside and is all there is. We don't need to suppose that everything needs to be ordered and controlled by some Higher Power. On the contrary, very complex ordered systems like an animal body or a language can evolve here below, just by trial and error over a long period.

This world is outsideless. Everything is immanent. More than that, we humans have been the only makers of our own language, and even (astonishingly, but think about it) our own minds. We made language and the system of indexical pronouns in such a way that each of us can and does construct her own subjectivity within language. The feeling of your own subjectivity is built up within you by the constant motion of language, both inside you and in and out of you. We really did make ourselves in that sense, and we also constructed within our language our entire world-picture and all our knowledge. We made our own minds: we made our world. *Our* world is *the* world.

People whose thinking is still influenced by traditional theology may still find all this strange and paradoxical. Yet it's obvious, really. Take a look at a ten-million-volume university library, or, more impressively, at some of the vast databases in which the whole of scientific literature is nowadays stored. We human beings have ourselves created all that, and surprisingly recently, too. Only two or three hundred years ago human beings were still amazingly ignorant. People knew almost nothing about how everything began, about how human beings have evolved, and about how our language and culture have evolved and now work. They had to be content with a primitive picture of all reality as having been created by God, and of all truth as subsisting eternally in the mind of God, who communicates to us, by illumination or revelation, everything that we most need to know. That was their myth, and it seemed to them to work well enough: indeed, theology gave them almost the only ideas they had about how to do research and build up a body of knowledge. As they saw it, beyond the human world here below was the eternal world that religion calls the Mind of God, and it is from that eternal divine Mind that all truth has come down to us.[26] Jews, Christians, and Muslims all believed that God had personally composed the scriptures in heaven, and then had caused them to be dictated to us. That was the paradigm case of knowledge and how we got it.

Today, however, everything has come down to earth. The Mind of God has turned into those great databases and libraries in which all of knowledge is stored, and the immanent, ubiquitous Spirit of God has turned into a ceaseless, humming, world-wide web of communication that links us all the time. Systematic theology, built out of the scriptural revelation, is no longer our prime (and almost our only) example of a great organized body of knowledge. We now have many more and vastly greater examples that we have built up all by ourselves and without any supernatural aid. Today the old split between the world below and the world above — also known as the intelligible world of philosophy, or the heavenly world of religion — is closed. There is only one world, and it is this world, our world, the world that we alone have appropriated, 'named', and set in order. Today the old sacred world of religion simply coincides with the ordinary everyday world, the world of ordinary language. Religion no longer has, no longer needs, a separate world, a separate vocabulary and way of thinking of its own. Its world is just the everyday world, our world. And it no longer has a separate divine life of its own, distinct from the natural biological and historical life of human beings. There is only one 'life', and it is a finite continuum with no outside. And the theology we actually live by is given by the idioms in ordinary language which show how we currently think of and manage our lives.

A corollary of this discussion: all traditional religion now rests upon, and struggles to inculcate, a profoundly false form of consciousness. Sadly, we have to confess that conservative faith's prolonged refusal to modernize it now leads it to do much more harm than good.

樂 樂 樂 樂 樂

The growing emphasis upon our emotional lives in my recent thinking has caused much concern in some quarters. Am I turning into a woman? people ask incredulously.

The question is in fact quite a good one, for even in these post-feminist times 'chick lit' and 'chick flicks' — current slang for novels and films produced chiefly by and for women and reflecting a woman's view of the world — remain highly popular. Feminists themselves readily acknowledge — or rather, claim with pride — that there certainly is such a thing as a woman-centred view of life, in which one lives immersed in one's emotions. Men of around, or up to half a generation above, one's own age exist chiefly as 'ancillaries' to women, and as possible objects of love. Unfortunately, however, woman's absorption in the life of the emotions is the source of her traditional 'weakness', for it makes her vulnerable to suffering, tears, victimhood, and depression. In the past, male-dominated society sought to protect her by secluding her within marriage and domestic life. But this was not a good remedy: in fact it sealed her up in a permanent state of powerless victimhood, and modern woman has rightly rejected it. She has moved out into the world of public life and economic activity, and to enable herself to function happily in the world of work and public service she is demanding various changes in working conditions and in power relations. So successful has she been in these respects that already in the great conurbations of the modern West women are doing rather better than men. One profession after another has become predominantly female. The balance of power is shifting, rapidly.

What is noticeable in this account is the extent to which many modern feminists still accept, and make a virtue of, the doctrine that the two sexes are differently constituted. Woman lives by the heart; she is the creature of her emotions and needs to talk about them. And man? He is taught from an early age to control his emotions, whether by bottling them up or by simply neglecting them. He learns that his conduct in the public world must be guided by 'reason', which means that he is expected in his work and in his public activity to be guided by considerations of efficiency and prudence alone. In his view, any indulgence of his emotions must be within socially approved limits and relegated to his leisure time. Elizabeth Barrett Browning has a poem, 'A Man's Requirements', that makes the point here neatly and sardonically. In rather unctuous language adapted to her sensitivity, a man's voice demands from his woman her total devotion, promising in return that at some time in the future (when his many other commitments permit) he hopes to be able to give her about half of his own attention.

The modern feminist is not so very different from her Victorian predecessor. She still regards the two sexes as being differently constituted. Woman lives in her emotions. She is more preoccupied than a man usually is with her self-presentation — dress, grooming, good health, the state of her feeling-life — but in our late-modern world these preoccupations look like strengths rather than weaknesses. Nowadays a woman lives five years longer than a man, and outperforms a man in most areas of life. City life is to a considerable extent already feminized. In this context you may if you wish see my own growing 'emotivism' as an attempt to catch up. The Y chromosome doesn't change much, and modern masculinity is finding it difficult to evolve quickly enough. The new weaker sex needs to look at the remarkable success of women during the past half century, and to learn a few things from it about how we need to change. Perhaps we are already learning: men are becoming more concerned about what Foucault called 'the care of the self'[27] — which includes everything from clothes and grooming to paying close attention to one's own state of mental health. In that phrase, of course, 'mental' is an old-fashioned word for what we now speak of more accurately as our emotional well-being. The mind is the emotions.

From classical antiquity men have inherited a disciplinarian view of the self. One should strive for self-mastery, bringing the senses, the emotions, and spiritedness (or anger: *thumos*) under the monarchical government of 'reason'. People under the influence of this ideal have often believed that lifelong celibacy is possible and even admirable, that women are relatively 'weak', and that ease and pleasure are to be scorned — in this life, at least. But we now have good reason to repudiate such ideas. To be happier and live longer, men should learn from women a few things about the care of the self.

There is a further corollary of these remarks. In my account of religion I have retained the traditional doctrine that religious feeling is a kind of sublimation of sexual feeling. By a sublimation, though, I do not mean a spiritualization. Rather, religious feeling is libido that has become an open, generous, non-fixated, and non-self-regarding love of the world and joy in life. It is 'divine' love in the sense of being an objectless, nondiscriminating, and universal disposition — **loving It All.**

Now, if it remains true — as it has been for millennia — that there is a close relationship between religious and sexual feeling, then current debates about what sexual feeling is, and how it works rather differently in men, in women, and in non heterosexuals, are of much ethical and religious interest. This is another topic that we have neglected, but it peeks out of today's talk about 'women's spirituality' and 'gay spirituality'.

樂 樂 樂 樂 樂

Since the days of Kant and Hegel (and that currently rather neglected figure Karl Marx) Western thought has gradually given up all forms of the idea that our world, the world of human history and everyday life, is sustained and guided from a point outside it. In the older 'platonic' or 'metaphysical' scheme of thought, our world was a world of mere visible appearances. It was a very unsatisfactory and unstable world, and to orient yourself within it you had to look beyond it to the greater, invisible real world of eternal forms and standards. This greater world Beyond was philosophy's counterpart of the traditional supernatural world of religion. It governed the lower world in which we live: in it we had our first origin, and in it we will we hope find our last End.

The end of metaphysics, after Kant and Hegel, Feuerbach and Marx, is the end of realistically understood supernatural belief and the arrival of the age of the popular newspaper, the novel, liberal democratic politics, and ordinary life. Everything is immanent and humanly formed, including all the standards by which we measure and evaluate things. There is only our ordinariness and our ordinariness is outsideless. It is the only bedrock we have now, and even the only bedrock we need. There is no higher world beyond ordinariness, and there is no deeper order in which ordinariness is grounded. Ordinariness is all there is, and its measure is ordinary language because ordinary language is precisely and exactly tailored to ordinary life. Ordinary language is the currency of ordinariness — which is why one of the best ways to study ordinariness is simply to study ordinary language, seeking to understand how it works, what kind of world its use builds, and what it shows us about persons, personal relationships, and the course of our life.

All this is very straightforward, when ordinary language is relaxed, and on its home ground; but our everyday speech has also a very important, but oddly neglected, creative leading edge, which we see at the points where bold and provocative new metaphors and idioms are being introduced.[28] The best example of such a leading edge in ordinary language that I have found is the two hundred or so striking and quasi-religious life-idioms that have entered the language in the past forty years. It seems that this is the area in which we are presently developing a new world view and religious outlook. I collected a good new idiom a few hours before writing these words: **high on life**, meaning (roughly) exhilarated, confident, *engagé*, with a suggestion that it is possible for us to find our ordinary lives thrilling, if we can but learn to **love life** enough and **commit ourselves to life** sufficiently and wholeheartedly. The blessed are not people who inhabit another world: they are simply those who live ordinariness most intensely.

In these striking and often rather paradoxical phrases we get a glimpse of ordinary language's theology, or at least of the religious message that it is just now preaching to us. **Get a life!** it says: **Life is for living** — which I take to signify that that rather nebulous entity **the meaning of life** is not a piece of secret information about a great supernatural purpose that is being fulfilled through our lives, but is something that is quite evident to people who are **living life to the full**.

So far, I am suggesting that in our new and completely secular world everything has returned into ordinariness. Ordinariness itself now needs to be studied seriously, for it has become basic and guiding in the way that the supernatural world used to be. In fact, it is as if the whole sacred world of religion simply coincides with the world of ordinary life. True religion is to be in love with and utterly at peace with ordinary life.

However, there are problems. We still perceive our life-world as being subject to its traditional 'metaphysical' limits of contingency, temporality, and finitude. Being contingent, nothing is completely safe and reliable and everything is liable to accident and misfortune; being temporal, everything passes by in one direction irrevocably, and passes away forever; and being finite, everything succumbs eventually to death or dissolution. Nothing lasts forever, nothing is completely secure, and death will terminate even the greatest love. Thus we are still liable to see our human life-situation as being relatively limited and imperfect, even though there is no longer any perfect world with which to contrast it. This lingering discontent was traditionally relieved by lyric poetry, which gave us painfully sweet metaphors of life's loveliness and transience.

But the question is, Can religion do any better than that? In the new worldview that I have so often described, there is no supernatural order. Religion cannot promise that any rescue mission will come to our aid from another world. All this, around us, is all there is. In which case the language of religion, its rituals and its practice, must all be a matter simply of metaphors. In which case, again, the comfort that religion gives surely cannot be any more substantial than the comfort given by poetry; and if so, why bother with it?

Earlier, I claimed that tragic conflict between different impulses in our own makeup can be resolved by the great healing and reconciling symbols of religion. Perhaps. Religious rituals may help us to get ourselves together internally, but what we are presently discussing is something much greater and utterly intractable. For the 'metaphysical' limits of life ensure that all our loves, even the greatest of all, must end in eternal separation. And we all know already that for the one who survives there is no consolation: everything that can be said is a wretched cliché. Neither religion nor art can offer any amelioration, which prompts an uncomfortable thought: the return of everything into ordinariness in the late-modern world is in many ways a great blessing. We are delivered from the illusions of metaphysical and supernatural belief, and are able to say a wholehearted Yes to life, just as it is. I am reasonably confident that the individual who practises solar living will be able, when the time comes, to journey all the way into death without fear or regret. But, on the downside, there are the eternal partings that we must all of us experience at one time or another. They stand out more intractable and starkly unconsoled than ever.

That is a novel and strange thought. Tradition always claims to be complete and sufficient, and so does every great religious system. But my religion is incomplete: it has one great surd that I have no wish to disguise. Even the leading pessimist Schopenhauer finishes his great book with a little flourish of pseudo-consoling verbal legerdemain, an unexpected show of weakness in such a major figure.[29] We must not make that mistake again. So: there is a tragic bit of life that I cannot tame or domesticate or incorporate into my system, and that is that. People have of course always claimed that the practice of religion — its rituals, its great symbols, its teachings — offers consolation in such a case. But in the past such consolation as people were able to find in religion depended upon illusory beliefs. So I must simply acknowledge that one may at any time suffer an absolute loss for which there is not and cannot be any consolation. It's the price of love.

樂 樂 樂 樂 樂

Let me quote an example — a very tough one for me. Towards the end of their lives my parents were around eighty years old and had been married fifty-nine years. We realized that they had come to the stage at which each of them lived only for the other's sake. One day soon, the blow would fall. It did: I received a telephone call from my mother and reached the old family home in the evening, an hour or two after my father had died. I went up to see my mother. She was stricken beyond any possibility of comfort or consolation, My father had died as he'd always wished to die, quickly and almost painlessly. A brain haemorrhage. I've had it too, so I know exactly what it is: a sudden headache, a thumping, pulsing sensation, and one passes out. Not bad for him; but my mother would never recover. She would sink into depression with nothing left to live for and take five years to die.

My father died on about February 9, 1992. In the glove locker of his car was his last valentine card for my mother, already purchased. He was an efficient man. Should we give it to her, on his behalf?

Some things are simply unbearable. For some things there is no consolation, and no religion or philosophy ought any longer to pretend otherwise. Despite the conventional way of discussing these things, one's own death is no great problem. Solar living conquers the fear of death. I know. But there are certain other people whose death will be a blow from which one cannot recover. I know my own official answer: it is the practice of 'solar loving', love that fully acknowledges its own transience, both choosing one's love and giving her up afresh each day.[30] That is the answer; the only possible answer. I know my own teaching — so I should, at my age — but I fear that in the event it may turn out to be of no help at all, even to me.

There is only one thing left to say. We are transient, mortal beings. Love is the best thing we have in our lives, and is what, for most of us, does most to make our lives worthwhile. But we pay a price for it: it comes to an end. There are eternal partings for which there is absolutely no consolation. Since, however, we wouldn't be without love, we'll buy it even at that killing price.

樂 樂 樂 樂 樂

There is room for argument about exactly when it was that Western culture ceased to be based upon religion, but many historians would opt for a date around the year 1720 or so. By then, people had digested the sheer magnitude of Newton's achievement. They knew that they were witnessing not a mere Revival of Learning, but a decisive surpassing of antiquity.[31] The traditional location of all intellectual authority in the past was at an end. The belief in progress appeared, and people began to reconstruct all knowledge around the human subject, its maker. The idea that all truth exists first in the Mind of God, and by God is communicated to the minds of humans, was quietly discarded, and at the same time people began to give up appealing to God to underpin human knowledge by guaranteeing its objectivity. The whole business of gaining knowledge was secularized. You no longer had to perform religious acts of self-purification: all you needed was the right method. Western thought began to move away at last from Augustine and Plato, and 'the naturalizing of epistemology' began.

As Nature was valued more highly, the human feeling-response to experience attracted more attention. Beginning with Shaftesbury's *Inquiry Concerning Virtue* of 1699, an influential English school of moral philosophers, the 'moral sense' school, attempted to naturalize ethics by basing their accounts of it on our natural feelings or sentiments of benevolence, sympathy, and so forth. In what is popularly regarded as the Age of Reason, the most striking innovation is the extent to which major figures such as Rousseau and Hume regarded the human being as a creature of natural feeling. But the whole period was like that. Religion was for the first time coming to be seen in terms of human feeling, as 'religious experience', as religious feeling, and as what we would today call 'spirituality'. Art, similarly, and again for the first time, was coming to be seen in terms of aesthetic experience — that is, in terms of the feeling-response that the artwork provokes in us. The famous turn to Nature in English landscape gardening and folly-building — evidence of which we see at places like Great Badminton, Cirencester Park, and Stourhead — shows the garden becoming a theatre of special effects, designed to activate particular emotions in the visitors who are taken round it. And at the same time, in the early eighteenth century, modern humanitarianism begins in figures such as Thomas Coram, whose Foundling Hospital was visited by parties of upper-class ladies who wished to learn and to cultivate the highly fashionable new sentiment of philanthropy.

Modern commentators are apt to ridicule the psychological tourism of the early eighteenth-century gentry who visited everything from grottoes to madhouses in order to experience interesting new frissons of feeling, but those were the days when the modern human sensibility was being invented. Until then the chief concern of life for many people had been their relation to God, and they typically knew themselves only as they appeared when they conducted a close *religious* self-examination. Divine law was the standard by which they assessed themselves, and this particular criterion did not exactly do much to encourage either a high valuation of, or even any interest in, the passions. But now during the eighteenth century there begins a large-scale turn to Nature, to an increasingly autonomous humanism, to human subjectivity, and to the emotions. As in literature the novel and naturalistic drama become more prominent, more and more it begins to look as if, for the average person, life's chief task has become that of gaining a better understanding of human psychology, human emotional life, the nature and the development of human personality, and human relationships. Traditionally, women have always given these topics more attention, and they have been particularly prominent amongst the writers, the subject matter, and the readership of novels. Men have lagged somewhat behind. (And indeed the Y chromosome that carries the distinctively male, sex-linked characteristics is the bit of the human genome that changes least. Unreconstructed maleness is the nearest thing to a constant that there is in human nature — an interesting scientific footnote to the Augustinian doctrine that Original Sin is transmitted in the male line.)

So we new men — if one can still be 'new' in any sense, at my age —

are trying to catch up. We have fallen somewhat behind in the course of what has been a very long historical process of psychological enrichment. That is part of my apologia for my 'emotivism'. The other part is to point out that by using the term emotivism I do not at all mean to suggest irrationalism. Rather the opposite, for what men think of as women's 'radar', or 'intuition', or 'instinct', or just plain suspiciousness, is all that men can usually see of a way of attending to one's own feeling-life that treats it as being itself a sort of sense organ, and as being at least incipiently cognitive. By habitually neglecting their own emotions, men have been missing out on the fact that our differential feeling-responses to things, situations, and persons can be, and in the case of women usually are, extremely sensitive — or even alarmingly perceptive. This is the first and most general level at which the whole world of our experience gets differentiated, structured, and coloured. We are talking here of intimation, hunch, mood, **atmosphere**, and **feeling that**; a delicate area in which women's thoughts are moving much of the time as they form hypotheses, drop hints, and ask probing questions, generally checking up on their nearest and dearest, and working out **the lie** (in North America, **the lay) of the land** — the current moral topography of a relationship or a situation.

Have I made myself clear? I am talking about the sort of thing that nowadays is called **emotional intelligence**, about a delicately emotive way of thinking about the intentions, plans, and feelings of others which is almost habitual to women, but of which men have known relatively little. What John Henry Newman described as the 'illative sense'[32] may represent a gay man's attempt to introduce it into philosophy. For my part, I am suggesting that the whole subject is of great interest and deserves more attention than it has so far received (from men, that is). When we live immersed in our own feeling-life, when we treat our own delicate feeling-responses as proto-cognitive, when we frame hypotheses on the basis of them, and check them out with light but searching questions and hints — when, in short, we move in all this highly female territory we are very well placed to grasp something of what 'thought' is, how it first evolved, and what it is *for*. All of which is particularly interesting to someone like me, who for religious reasons seeks a thoroughly naturalistic and one-level account of things that does not need to divide the human being between different realms — inner and outer, mental and physical, or rational and emotional. Such dualistic contrasts, either within the self or between the self and the not-self, always threaten to become acutely painful. They are obstacles to salvation: for unless they can be closed, the religious kind of happiness that I seek cannot be attained. So I like the idea of **living by the heart** or 'thinking with one's feelings', and I want to take it further.

樂 樂 樂 樂 樂

So accustomed are we in the modern West to seeing religious belief as irrational that it has become hard to remember how exceedingly rationalistic the West's basic religious concepts once were. What distinguished a human being from an animal was the human's possession of a rational soul. The soul was a finite spiritual substance made in the image of God, and so a little counterpart of God. Being thus godlike, the soul will find its highest happiness in eternally contemplating the God who is both its Origin and its End. In short, the best and most fulfilling way of life is the life of reason, as lived by a philosopher or a monk.

In retrospect, it is evident that our tradition was dominated for around two millennia by an extreme supernaturalism of reason. Our rationality was nothing to do with our biology: it was a special supernatural endowment, bestowed individually upon each one of us, that made us capable of communing with God. Reason should rule our bodies and our passions, orienting us towards the attainment of our final happiness in God — that is, in the eternal world.

You will see that, as I have been arguing that religious happiness must now be sought not in the eternal spiritual world but simply in this life, this body, and this world, so I am now arguing that we should change over from a monkish to a more 'female' conception of reason— a conception that is rooted in our biology and in the emotions. We should give up thinking of our reason as a little God-implanted pilot in our heads that wants to guide us back to our last home in the eternal world. Instead we should see reason, in the sense simply of thinking, as the manoeuvrings of our own feelings and desires, trying to secure their own fulfilment and our happiness by working out **how other people tick**, and so managing our relationships with them satisfactorily. In which case, we may even conclude that female-type reason — 'emotional intelligence' — is actually more up-to-date and *more rational* than traditional male-type, 'sky-pilot' rationality!

There is a supplementary argument for breaking with the traditional connection of reason with the individual soul and the eternal world. It is, I suggest, a matter of observation that truly rational individuals are scarce. In practice, most people encounter rationality not as an individual endowment but as a great public and social creation upon which we depend, and within which we live. An excellent example is the civil law: ordinary folk are seldom short of their own ideas about who's to blame when something goes wrong and how severely he should be punished, but we all know that the law teaches us things about what is to be admissible in evidence and how to weigh it, about responsibility and culpability and so on, that are far, far superior in rationality to anything that an individual is likely to be able to come up with on her own. In this case, then, the civil law is the great social institution that is the nursery of reason: it teaches us who live within it how to be rational. And something similar is also true of a few other and related institutions, such as language and scientific knowledge, which also illustrate the important general principle that what has been, and still is being, worked out and tested publicly is likely to be much superior in rationality and consistency to any merely individual production. Rationality, linguistic meaning, truth and justice are all of them best regarded as public and communal productions. These things are not naturally inherent in human individuals, but are products of the public realm, and are taught to individuals by the way things are done in the public realm.

This argument has some bearing upon my method of collecting and studying philosophically and religiously interesting idioms in ordinary language. Many people have remarked on the striking fact that our language is much brighter than the individuals who use it. But gifted individual writers who are — or seem to be — masters of language have a way of describing stock idioms and phrases as *clichés*, and avoiding them ostentatiously. That is why I have found it so hard to make my point about the wisdom that is in ordinary language. But why are writers like Martin Amis so very hard on clichés?[33] Are they perhaps snobbishly overeager to distance themselves from the rest of us, whose experience is rather that so-called clichés are, in fact, often very beautiful and instructive?

樂 樂 樂 樂 樂

For some years now I have been using the phrase 'democratic philosophy'. By it I mean to suggest that the traditional Western ideas of the great writer who remakes language, and the great thinker, the philosophical genius who single-handedly remakes the world in thought, are now somewhat out of date. In our time society is large scale, with an enormous division of labour. It is also highly communicative and fast changing: new words, new phrases, new ideas are diffused at a rapid pace. Under these new conditions we should spend less time admiring the tiny number of creative individuals and much more time studying philosophical and religious change at the 'mass' or public level. I am suggesting that we have a soundly objective and rational way of doing this, by collecting, dating, and interpreting the striking new phrases that are all the time nowadays being introduced into our common speech. When we collect and interpret this material we are dealing with stuff that we all of us know, that has already made its way amongst us, and is publicly established.

Martin Amis's criticisms imply that the 'democratic' method of attending closely to ordinary language and stock phrases will not find material of any great intellectual interest. Clichés are lazy and stale, a substitute for thought — so it is said. But in fact when we study the new stock phrases as they arrive in the language, we are often surprised by how up-to-date they are. Very often we discover that quite daring new philosophical ideas, which remain sharply controversial in academic circles, have been part of ordinary language for years. Thus the conservative intellectuals who denounce anti-realism, postmodernism and relativism fail to notice that these cultural movements are already built into everyday speech — for example, in the very striking use of 'perception' to mean 'interpretation', which has been around for at least one decade, and probably two.

For another example, think how often we see someone battling against obstacles that appear to him to be real and objective, and say to him things like **you are your own worst enemy**, or **you make life hard for yourself**. What he regards as being objectively real and obdurate seems to us to be a projection, a phantom enemy. Ordinary language is often sceptical even about people's ability to see things that are **right under their noses**. **There are none so blind as those who won't see**, we say, **People hear what they want to hear**. That we are ourselves (whether individually, or collectively) the makers of our worlds is implied by many idioms like **He lives in a world of his own**.

In a nutshell, I was brought up to believe that the ordinary person's philosophy is a form of naïve realism — about perception, about the world of fact, and about objective truth. But ordinary language nowadays tells a quite different story.

※ ※ ※ ※ ※

Here is an elegant and powerful statement of the ordinary person's anti-realism, as it is typically expressed today. It is taken from Mr John Virgo's commentary on the 2003 Embassy World Snooker Championship, held in Sheffield, and broadcast in early May on BBC2. The eventual winner, Mark Williams, was having a bad patch, and the balls were running unluckily for him. Virgo said — and I ran for paper, and wrote the words down on the spot — what Williams must do to get out of his losing streak:

> He must put out of his mind the thought that the gods are against him — even if it appears to be so. In the end, it's never fate: it's always you.

The speaker, the topic, the occasion — all were quite impeccably 'ordinary'. In that context, Virgo's words are a splendidly lucid and convincing statement of the non-realist point of view. All those supposedly 'objective' realities out there, against which we are tempted to see ourselves as battling, are phantoms conjured up by our own weakness. We will begin to do better when we say firmly to ourselves: 'It's never fate: it's always you'. That is why ordinary people and ordinary language praise courage and fighting spirit above almost all other virtues.

粼 粼 粼 粼 粼

Some years ago a friend who is a Roman Catholic nun in Australia sent me a postcard. I looked at it and blinked. It was a reproduction of one of Claude Monet's river paintings of the 1890s. Everything depicted in it was a transient effect: vegetation hanging over water, light falling down from above and reflected up again from the water surface, patches of shadow and areas of bluish haze. As with all such paintings, there was no single, clear focal point. Instead, the world is seen as something like a shimmering magical illusion that pulls the eye. One is drawn forward, out into the world thus seen, and scattered blissfully into endless, empty peace.

I love such paintings. They make me feel like an old Chinese sage contemplating landscape and murmuring that 'Impermanence is also Buddha-nature'. But coming from a Roman Catholic nun, the postcard made about as heretical a statement as can well be imagined. Official Roman doctrine and spirituality remain to this day intensely platonic. They tell us to turn away from the transient things of this world which deceive the soul by pleasing the senses. We should give our whole attention to the things that alone are truly valuable, the invisible things of the Eternal World above: God, the angels, the saints, spiritual values, and the cardinal virtues. The only sort of beauty that is good for the soul is the kind of beauty that is incorruptible and invisible. As for the ephemeral beauties of this world, they are a pagan deception. They are tempting, certainly, but in the end they always let us down and leave us with dust and vain regrets.

I still do not know whether, in choosing the Monet picture to send to me, my friend was making a conscious ideological statement or not. I think she has long been aware of feminism, and the card may have been declaring: 'I like everything that is as transient, volatile, sensuous, shimmering, and worldly as a woman's feelings'. She may have been saying something like that, in the knowledge that I would warmly agree, and in full awareness of how profoundly feminism subverts traditional Catholic/platonic values. But then again, she may simply have picked up in a shop a picture-postcard that she liked. I don't know — but it is reasonable to guess that she doesn't scorn transient earthly pleasures and beauties quite as confidently as Catholics did until the late seventeenth century.

For my part I have claimed often enough that we can and must reverse the old platonic valuations, and should criticize the surviving scraps of vocabulary that preserve them. For example, we should insist that there is nothing wrong with the theatre just as such, and therefore one shouldn't talk as if all acting is playacting or hypocrisy (Greek: *hupokrites*, 'actor'); there's nothing wrong with having volatile feelings, and therefore they shouldn't always be characterized as fickle; and there's nothing wrong with the beauty of surfaces, and therefore we shouldn't be so quick to condemn something for being superficial. Similarly, we should certainly not use the word emotional to mean either drunk or highly embarrassing. Our language still contains too many relics of the extreme long-termist rationalism (not to mention the sexism) of the past. We should bring them out into the open and give them a good kicking, in order to prepare ourselves for a new and better religious outlook and way of life.

The new path is the one that at different times I have called *ecstatic immanence*, *glory*, the *mysticism of secondariness*, and *solar living* — and a few other things too. I have pushed different new phrases at different times, in the hope of one day finding a term that people will promptly understand, like, and take up. The point of the terms is that one gives up all ideas of real being and real value as being somehow timeless or 'absolute'. Instead, one learns to see the world as outpouring, energetic, temporal process, and oneself as simply a part of the general flux. One learns to say, I just *am* my own **passing**, my own transient life. I am not a basically immortal being who sees all transient things as dying on him, and slipping away from him. On the contrary, I am *myself* transient: *I* am passing away *too*, at just the same speed as all those other transient things. I am *with them*, and my heightened awareness of my own mortality actually *enhances* my feeling for all other transient things. Hence Walter de la Mare's fine lines urging us to love the world as much as possible, and right up to the very end: 'Look thy last on all things lovely / Every hour'.[34] At my age you remember those words each spring, as you see the first Brimstone, Comma, and Small Tortoiseshell once again.[35] One feels intense affection for the way these lifelong friends keep coming back, afresh and as lovely as ever each year. In this recognition there is also a *memento mori*, and a stab of anguish. But that stab of anguish at the heart of all mortal love is what gives to our life its peculiarly human poignancy and intensity, and we wouldn't really be without it.

So I have at times suggested that we can best cope with metaphysical evil by forcibly revaluing it. There cannot be any other solution to the religious problem but the one that calls upon us to commit ourselves unreservedly to our own transient lives, and to love all the other creatures and beauties that are as transient as we are. As we do this our idea of the self changes: We are not immortal beings making a brief passage through this dangerous and changeable world and trying to protect our souls from getting soiled during the journey through earthly life: no, we are more like candles — we live by burning, we should burn brightly, and when we are burnt out we are simply gone, snuffed out. Selfhood is like a theatrical performance: it is enacted before others and in our relations with them, and it lasts a finite time. When it is done, it is over. Till then, put on a good show! We have only our own time, and there are no retakes. **Give it all you've got** while it lasts!

In my programme for the complete reinvention of religion I have argued that since the turn to ordinary lay and domestic life began — perhaps in the Low Countries and in the towns along the Rhine, and perhaps in the fifteenth century, or (if you prefer) in seventeenth-century Holland — since then, the focus of religious attention has gradually moved to this life. Increasingly the realm in which people hope to find eternal happiness is simply that of everyday life in the here and now, and we see the new outlook arriving in the growing popularity of idioms that ascribe sanctity or inviolability to marriage, domestic life, the home, privacy, and even (eventually) to individual human rights. As we get older we become more and more aware of the new life, idioms that urge us to **live for the moment**, to **live life to its fullest**, to **take each day as it comes**, and to **make the most of it while it lasts**. So, as religion returns fully into this life, it increasingly needs to take the form of all-out solar living. And I firmly believe that solar living works. By practising it, we can become completely reconciled to, and at ease with, the 'human condition' — by which I mean simply the fact that the world is a contingent, temporal process and that everything is transient. We are simply part of **It All**. Solar spirituality is an all-out attempt to learn, and to practise as religion, our own unity with the general burning and burning out of everything. And it works! It really can make us happy with life and unafraid of death, which is the main job that our religion is meant to do for us.

So far, so good. But a major caveat needs to be entered. Traditional religion promised *absolute* security — a universal restoration and a state of beatitude that would endure for all eternity and could never be threatened. But I can't promise any such thing, and I have already pointed out that although by solar living I really can completely conquer the fear of the Void and my own death, there remain a number of other people, any one of whom may perhaps die suddenly at any time, and whose loss would inflict on me a blow from which I could not recover. Thus my this-worldly religion cannot promise the complete and final security that the old religion offered. A small contingent shift in the chemistry of your brain —

and your state of eternal happiness is gone. Nowadays we live for around eight decades, and a substantial percentage of us face the prospect of a very unpleasant last few years of decrepitude. In these last years, all the effort of decades of religious practice during which we have tried to make ourselves into people who love life and their neighbours and can say Yes to the human condition — all that effort collapses as we are reduced to wreckage by Parkinson's, Alzheimer's, or strokes.

There is no permanent victory to be promised anymore. There is only transience. One mustn't make any long-term claims, because there are no long-term guarantees. Religion itself is only a transient effect, too. So: I can practise my solar living now, and say that so long as I'm able to keep renewing it all the time then, Yes, it works … *now*. But that's all: hence the attraction of those philosophies that have suggested that we should live as if only the present moment is real. And to those who will complain that my account gives an 'inadequate' answer to the problem of evil I have to retort that the basic facts of life, contingency, and death remain the same on all accounts.

樂 樂 樂 樂 樂

The old faiths are all crumbling fast just now, and it is very important indeed that we should encourage people to believe that they can and must step clear of all the dying vocabularies, go back to the beginnings of philosophy and religious thought, and start afresh. All we want is simple, clear, and honest religious thinking in the everyday vocabulary of ordinary people. We should forget the technical vocabulary of our own ancestral religion, whatever it is, and confine ourselves to ordinary language, the idioms of which already contain our basic common philosophy of life and religious outlook. All we have to do is to dig that common faith out and to stay close to it. We should speak as simply as Mr Virgo himself: '**In the end, it's never fate: it's always you**'.[36] Simple, so simple that no professional theologian or philosopher would ever dare to speak so clearly. He'd be ridiculed.

Why is contemporary professional religious and philosophical thought so weak, obscure, and confused? One of the main reasons is that we are no longer able to state clearly where we are trying to get to or what we are trying to achieve. At one time this question was the very first that the Catechism posed: Calvin, for example, opened his Geneva Catechism of 1541 with the admirably straightforward question and answer: 'What is the chief end of human life?' — 'To know God'. A little more fully, the Westminster Larger Catechism of 1648 begins: Q. What is the chief and highest end of man? — A. Man's chief and highest end is to glorify God, and fully to enjoy him for ever.[37]

It is odd that a question that could once be raised and answered so early and straightforwardly should now be causing us such difficulties. We flounder confusedly in our debates about **the meaning of life**. What happened?

The answer, briefly, is that thought about the goal of the religious life and the goal of the life of philosophy formerly seemed to make sense because in prescientific times a teleological style of thinking about *everything* was usual. Not only 'man' but everything had been made for a purpose, and so had a goal or 'chief end', towards which it naturally gravitated. But then with the triumph of mechanistic science all talk of purposiveness in nature was banished: events were henceforth to be explained as having been *pushed* by earlier events, their efficient causes, and there was to be no more talk of 'final causes' as 'pulling' events. In the closing lines of Dante's *Paradiso* the divine Love draws Dante's own heart and the turning Heavens in the same way, because God *pulls* all created things, hearts and stars alike.[38] Everything tries to imitate God by moving in its own way towards the special form of perfection that God has appointed for it. In that context, it seemed obvious that human life had a great and appointed End, and that religion would help you to attain it.

Aristotle had supplied many of the key ideas.[39] Each thing, he says, has its own End or *telos*, which is the good, for it. Therefore (somewhat illogically) *the* Good is 'that at which all things aim'. Our peculiar excellence as human beings is our rationality. Therefore the supreme good for us is that we shall at last arrive at an immediate, complete and supremely satisfying intellectual vision of the Good, absolutely. And we will know it 'absolutely' — just as it is — and forever.

What philosophy called 'the Good', then, is the final end of all desire, and the goal towards which in their various ways all things move. Our highest human fulfilment, for which we have been expressly designed, is to attain total, intuitive, timeless, and blessedness-giving knowledge of the Good. We'll get to this state when, in the language of religion, we at last see God face to face. Our last End is *objectively* the Vision of God, and *subjectively* the blessedness or eternal happiness that will fill us when we contemplate God.

So it was said. Everything in the universe was seen in teleological terms — that is, as gravitating towards its own appointed form of perfection. The advantage of the old teleological style of thinking was that it enabled you in a single account to describe both how everything is and what everything is striving to become. The is-question and the ought-question could both be dealt with in the same story. In the case of us humans, this meant that one narrative explained both our present factu-

ality and our exalted spiritual destiny. And when the whole world of
thought worked in that way it was easy for people to see and spell out
what was the ultimate goal and point of the religious life, of philosophy,
and indeed of human life quite generally.

Then came natural science, and the rather sudden expulsion from
Nature of all talk of final causes and purposiveness. It could no longer be
claimed that a thing's spiritual destiny was a built-in part of it. The whole
notion of the Vision of God as the supreme goal of our life as rational
beings faded quickly. All that was left was a few lines here and there in
the New Testament: from Jesus, 'Blessed are the pure in heart, for they
shall see God', and from St Paul, 'For now we see in a mirror dimly, but
then face to face'.[40] This sounds very evocative, but it is all too vivid an
example of the way religious language seems to mean something — but
then on closer inspection turns out to have told us nothing at all. For
God, being by definition infinite, simple, and bodiless, cannot be seen
and has no face. 'Seeing God' cannot be anything like the seeing that
opticians deal with, and where God is there is no light of the sort that
physicists theorize about. 'Seeing God face to face' is therefore an obscure
and highly metaphorical way of speaking about what it might be to enjoy
an immediate and entirely non-metaphorical intuition of the divine
essence. In short, there is a curious dissonance, or even contradiction,
between the linguistic expression 'seeing God face to face' and the timeless intellectual intuition of the divine essence that it purports to be
telling us about. The words seem comforting, but they tell us nothing.
And that is what is wrong with a large part of our received religious language. It is a deception. St Paul had an off day when he wrote that bit of
his *First Letter to the Corinthians*.

So far, however, I have let off St Paul a good deal too lightly. The
reasons why we have lost the old teleological way of thinking about everything, and in particular have lost the old metaphysical understanding of
what human reason is and of where it should look to find its supreme fulfilment, cut much deeper than I have yet indicated. For we think in language, and all our knowing is linguistically mediated. But in language —
and therefore also in the real world that our language gives us — everything is relative, shifting, temporal, and mediated. Everything is changing, secondary, and incomplete, and nothing can ever quite get to be
absolute, perfect, and final. This may all sound very unsatisfactory, but it
isn't really so, because it is only in an in-between and slipping-away sort
of world like ours that linguistic meaning and personal life are possible at
all. We cannot begin to imagine either total meaningfulness delivered all
at once, or timeless and unchanging personal life. It is not a bit surprising

that, as soon as he had grasped the Galileo-and-Descartes vision of a universe in ceaseless motion, Thomas Hobbes should have declared so forthrightly that there just cannot be such a thing as the Summum Bonum, the Highest Good, a state of absolute rest and timeless contemplative knowledge. We'll only ever get to be timeless and at rest when we are dead. Meanwhile, all life is ceaseless motion from beginning to end.[41] The old Aristotelian doctrine that we humans ache to come to rest forever in a state of timeless perfection is a deception, because that kind of knowledge never was and never will be on offer.

I have argued, then, that the main reason for the intellectual weakness of modern religion is that it can no longer say clearly what it wants, or where it is trying to get to. The necessary vocabulary is no longer available. The old objective goal of life, the Vision of God, has completely lost mindhold since the end of metaphysics, which occurred just after Hegel.

But what about the *subjective* end of life, beatitude or eternal happiness? Here we are talking about something that was always supposed to be a state of *ourselves*, and therefore ought surely to be more intelligible? Happiness will always be most readily linked, not with timelessness and rational necessity, but with 'hap', which is contingency. Happiness is not anything absolute or final, but always something that is secondary, epiphenomenal, or supervenient. It 'comes over' us or 'visits' us, *because* we are in love, on holiday, absorbed in creative work, briefly liberated from our usual cares, or whatever. In short, happiness never fitted very well into the old worldview, but it does fit into the modern picture of our life as an endless, outsideless, and contingent flux of interwoven events. A purely this-worldly account of religion ought surely to be able to give a satisfactory account of what religious happiness is. In short, I can be sure that the Vision of a (metaphysical) God was never really on offer; but I can be sure (and indeed, I am sure) that religious happiness in this life is verifiably attainable.[42]

樂 樂 樂 樂 樂

Many people are religious seekers. Sometimes they talk as if they are searching diligently in the supermarket of world religions for something they might want to buy: but how many of them have thought in any rigorous way about method? In 1637 René Descartes launched our modern critical style of thinking, which applies in pretty much the same way to philosophy, to science, and to historical subjects. He proposed his Method of Doubt.[43] Nothing was to be exempt from criticism, and everything that could be doubted, should be. It ought to be possible, in principle, to bring all our beliefs and assumptions to the light and expose each of them in turn to the sort of public testing and evaluation that is given to witnesses who are cross-examined in court. And, of course, not only must individual beliefs be clear and strong enough to survive critical examination, but also the systems of knowledge into which we assemble them must be similarly clear and coherent. We should never allow ourselves to be fobbed off with an argument to the effect that some belief or belief-system is too venerable, or too mysterious, or too great and authoritative to be criticisable.

One wonders immediately what would happen to religion if it were publicly subjected to a testing as minute and rigorous as Descartes proposes. Descartes himself had the same thought, and being a prudent man who had observed the fate of Galileo with some alarm, he expressly exempted religion. It was too sensitive a subject. Then, at least. But what would it be today for a modern seeker to embark upon a personal religious quest, armed with a rigorous critical method of (roughly) the type that Descartes himself proposed?

I propose the following maxims:

1. In religion, as in other subjects, *we should not accept any beliefs dogmatically*. No belief should be accepted because it is traditional, or because it is greatly venerated. In fact, we should not accept *any* secondhand or ready-made religious convictions.

2. Religious truth is of a kind that has to be personally appropriated and tested out ethically in one's own life. Hence the relevant test procedure differs somewhat from the ones used in science and history. The rule is that *the only true religious beliefs for you will be beliefs that you personally have appropriated and tested out in your own life, and have articulated and defended in conversation with others.*

3. (Corollary of 2.): From this it is clear that *the only true religious beliefs are heresies*, i.e. beliefs that one has chosen for oneself and made one's own, item by item. All orthodoxies, being presented to us for acceptance *en bloc* and ready-made, must be rejected. Besides, when did Tradition ever actually turn out to be right about anything at all?

4. For you, *true religion is your own voice* — a personal faith that you have evolved over a period of many years and have checked out rigorously in your living, and in your conversation with your own generation.

This account makes the religious quest much like the long struggle to find one's own voice and one's own personal style as an artist, a struggle which, in the case of the great Paris-school artists whom I have always admired, very commonly took about twenty years. My account is equally obviously autobiographical: I grew up in circles where 'faith' meant swallowing a religious belief-system whole, and it takes a long time to convince oneself of the superiority of a piecemeal approach. Hobbes comments sardonically:

> . . . it is with the mysteries of our religion as with wholesome pills for the sick, which, swallowed whole, have the virtue to cure; but chewed, are for the most part cast up again without effect.[44]

Hobbes is right to say that close, one-by-one 'chewing over' of the mysteries of religion has a strong demystifying effect. They gradually lose mindhold,[45] and fade away. But the few convictions that we do gradually find ourselves forming are all the stronger as a result. One is likely to end as a generally sceptical person with a cluster of tried-and-tested core religious convictions and values that one is content to live by and die in. And I am saying that such a person is very much better off than his contemporaries, who are still stuck in an unhappy and ambivalent relationship with a block-orthodoxy that they cannot wholeheartedly believe in anymore, but that they dare not explicitly abandon.

樂 樂 樂 樂 樂

The most extreme case is that of Eastern Orthodox Christianity (and, perhaps, Orthodox Judaism and perhaps Islam): Tradition always represents itself as *Holy* Tradition, a sacred and immutable plenum. It can never be changed, and it must always be swallowed whole. Even a minor deviation from it is treated as a major offence. And I am saying that this 'block' attitude to religious truth, which makes any programme of gradual, piecemeal reform impossible, is in fact the single most important point of conflict between Traditional religion and modern thought.

Surprisingly, Nietzsche agreed. Christianity, he says, is an integral system of thought.[46] Take away one item, and the whole thing starts to crumble. This seems odd, for ever since the initial gulf between Jesus and Paul has not Christianity always been an untidy cluster of conflicting strands of thought? I suspect that Nietzsche here makes one of his rare mistakes because of the way that the two versions of Christianity that he knew best, Roman Catholicism and Lutheranism, have each been sort-of unified by special factors. Roman Catholicism looks unified because of the way in which it makes everything else in Christianity serve its chief objective, the construction and maintenance of a single great pyramid of spiritual power that peaks in the Pope and at Rome; and Lutheranism makes Christianity look unified because of the way Martin Luther — perhaps Christianity's only major genius — has worked over everything and given it the characteristic flavour of his own marvellous mind. But these special unifying factors, namely Rome's great love of power and Luther's dialectics, only mask the fact that the religious materials that both of them inherited always were and still are miscellaneous.

For the purposes of our present argument it is enough for me to say that the critical religious enquirer must reject Tradition's 'block' view of religious truth, and insist upon the method that I have been proposing: a generally sceptical presumption, a piecemeal or item-by-item approach, and an existential-ethical method according to which one takes ideas to oneself and tests them out in one's personal life and one's conversation with others. Inevitably, one must become accustomed to living with a relatively 'thin' faith, which remains subject to review. But as is the case with natural science, this method, which seems so shot through with doubt, turns out eventually to deliver knowledge of a quality far, far superior to what one was given by the older dogmatic style of thinking and believing.

樂 樂 樂 樂 樂

When, barely a century ago, the teachings of Buddhism first became widely understood in the West, the reaction of many people was to suggest that Buddhism should be regarded not as a religion but rather as a philosophy of life. In English law, religion is to this day defined in terms of belief in and the worship of gods, but Buddhism is notably short on gods, and for that matter lacks the ideas of divine creation and divine revelation, miraculous intervention, and saving Grace that have meant so much to Christians. Instead, we hear a great deal about self-help.

It must be obvious that the view of religion that I have been putting forward owes something to ancient Greek philosophy and rather more to Buddhism. Some people are bound to think that I am presenting a recipe for constructing a personal philosophy of life rather than a system of religious belief, and they will say that at the very least, if I am to continue to claim the word *religion*, I need to define what I mean by a religious belief.

Evidently I do and must reject the developed Latin conception of faith that had come to prevail in the West by the early second millennium. Belief — or rather, faith — had come to be seen as the assent of the intellect to divinely revealed truths that are proposed to us by the church, which is their authorized keeper. These revealed truths are all about the supernatural world of God, the angels, and the blessed dead, and the dealings of that world with us. If we are to gain eternal happiness it is essential that we learn about what God has done to offer us the hope of eternal salvation, and about how we can avail ourselves of the offer.

This developed Latin account of faith is strongly intellectualist and lays great emphasis upon the role of the church in mediating divine truth and divine grace to us. Intellectual assent to the entire doctrine-system, on the basis of acceptance of the church's teaching authority, seems only prudent when we consider our own infinite interest in gaining personal salvation. But this whole account of faith is dependent upon the truth of at least two great presuppositions: 1) that there really *is* a greater, invisible and supernatural world beyond this world, from which there really has come a revelation of saving truth to us; and 2) that what the church proposes to us for our belief really is the very same One True Faith which was revealed, complete, at the beginning. And neither of these presuppositions can be defended. There is not now and there never was any One True Faith, which has been 'always the same' from the beginning, and will remain forever; and there is not any greater supernatural world beyond this world. Historical study has demolished the first presupposition, the belief in an historically unchanging, divinely given core truth in Christianity; and philosophical criticism has demolished the second, the belief in a controlling Sacred World, a more-real world behind the world that visibly appears to us. Our language gives us only one world, and it is this world, the world of everyday life. Like our language, this world of ours is a single continuum. It is all there is.

There is simply no room anymore for religious beliefs, either as history-proof unchanging divine truths, or as statements that somehow bridge the gap between two very different worlds. Instead, we should see religious beliefs as maxims to live by in *this* world, and we should see the various symbolic practices of religion as means by which we can resolve our various conflicting feelings about good and evil, and life and death. We are intensely emotional creatures: our lives are lives of feeling, and to be happy we need to forge at least a tolerably unified selfhood whose stream of feeling is continually awakened, drawn out, and channelled by powerful symbols and stories so that it can flow out into expression in productive activity and joy in life.

Religion, then, gives us symbols, stories, values, and ritual practices that can help us to live well and find eternal joy just in this, our transient life. And eternal happiness just is a steady surging outflow of joyous feeling. What makes this feeling religious is, first, that it is cosmic, because it is overflowing feeling for **It All**, for everything, for life; and second, that it has by the use of religious rites and symbols been purged of ressentiment and anxious self-concern (or 'egoism', or 'craving', or 'attachment'). One says, **Let it be**; 'All this, just as it is, is fine, and I don't want to change anything. **It is enough**.' Here is Virginia Woolf's *Mrs Dalloway*:

Life itself, every moment of it, every drop of it, here, this instant, now, in the sun, in Regent's Park, was enough. Too much, indeed.

I should comment that it so happens that, for biographical reasons, the religious stories and practices that I like, and that happen to work for me, are the Christian ones. So I am a practising Christian, even though I don't for a moment suppose that any of it is true in the standard dogmatic-realist Roman Catholic sense. But, given what today we perceive the human situation to be, Christianity is sort-of 'true', in the only sense in which *any* religious system is or can be true. It's true, in the sense that it works, or at least can be made to work, as religion. What more can one ask? So my view is in no way reductionist.

It follows that everything depends upon how you understand the contemporary human condition. In particular, what account should we give of the world, language, the self, feeling, and truth? If you still want to give something like the old Plato-to-Kant account, you'll say that I'm not a Christian, but merely some kind of perverse nihilist or postmodernist. But if you want to give something like the modern post-Hegel account, you'll see us-in-our-world as an immanent continuum. The world allegedly out there cannot actually be separated from our thinking about it, our language, and our feeling-life reflected in it. Everything is an interpretation. We need to learn to live without the older ideas of dogmatic truth and metaphysical (or objective) reality. And if you are of this latter party, you'll acknowledge that symbolic efficacy in helping us to sort out our feelings, live well, and be happy, is the only sort of truth left for a religious system to have. In those terms it may indeed be that Christianity, in my own version of it, works for me and is therefore true for me.

From this it follows in turn that we should now give up all 'strong' ideas of divine authority and exclusive truth. One set of symbols, practices, and values may work for me, and another set may work for you. We can be, and indeed we should be, thoroughgoing religious pluralists, and cheerfully eclectic. Why not? If over the years you have visited a number of Christian and Buddhist houses of religion in Europe and Asia, you will have been struck by the thought that the ways of life, the styles of spirituality, and the typical personalities you encounter can be surprisingly similar, despite the flat opposition of the two doctrine-systems involved. For example, Christian total reliance upon divine Grace is the exact opposite of the Buddhist reliance upon self-help, but it is not sensible to claim that only one of these two paths can lead to happiness, for manifestly both paths get there.

樂 樂 樂 樂 樂

As I have been writing this little book I have been aware (and the reader too has doubtless been aware) of an affinity with the young Wordsworth, whose poetry I have been reading for some years. It was in

Wordsworth as much as anyone that *the turn to ordinariness* began. The famous Preface which was printed in the second and later editions of *Lyrical Ballads* explains why:

> The principal object . . . proposed in these poems was to choose incidents and situations from common life, and to relate or describe them, throughout, as far as was possible in a selection of language really used by men . . . and . . . to make the incidents and situations interesting by tracing in them . . . primary laws of our nature.[47]

— and so on. The turn to ordinariness continues in such figures as Tolstoy and Wittgenstein, but in the little *Everyday Speech* books I took it very 'literally'. Perhaps influenced (I don't remember) by the Opies' famous and admirable books on the culture of childhood, I tried systematically to collect idioms from ordinary speech, and from them to extract something of the religion and philosophy of ordinariness.

A second point of affinity with Wordsworth is found in the fact that he was the first English poet to make a major topic of his own development — and of the development of the human personality generally — in its setting in nature and society. That he is by no means thinking only of the religious and moral training of the young is made apparent by the extraordinary and entirely novel titles given to many poems, such as the 'Influence of Natural Objects in Calling Forth and Strengthening the Imagination of Boyhood and Early Youth'. In brief, Wordsworth is of course intensely interested in sense-experience and in our emotional and imaginative development. The mind and the world almost make each other: Wordsworth verges on philosophical idealism, and loves to dwell on the interweaving of, and the blissful harmony between, our subjective life, the objective world, and the sounds of language. Just the precision and the *joie de vivre* can be breathtaking: in the poem just mentioned he remembers and evokes the sound of boys skating in the chilly gathering dusk on the lake at 6:00 pm on a November evening:

> All shod with steel
> We hissed along the polished ice . . .[48]

Sss! Third, there is of course also Wordsworth's *emotivism*, which need not be elaborated upon here. It is sufficient to say that for years I have thought that in figures like the young Schleiermacher and the young Wordsworth one glimpses wonderfully promising lines of thinking being opened up some two hundred years ago. Sadly, as it turned out, a great opportunity to renew European religion and culture was not exploited as fully as it should have been. Instead, both Schleiermacher and Wordsworth fell back into dull respectability and orthodoxy.

This comparison with Wordsworth's poetry prompts a question: How far can a religious outlook of the kind that I have described ever become truly communal? Surely what I have been describing is always a purely personal formation, something that an individual develops for herself over the years, a personal philosophy of life? Other people may find it interesting, as they may find Wordsworth's account of his own development interesting. They may perhaps be attracted to it, they may want to learn from it, or to borrow from it. But it remains a highly personal art-product, and they cannot literally adopt it as their own. In which case, my theory of religion (and, for that matter, the young Wordsworth's vision) cannot really be described as anything more than a personally evolved philosophy of life. In which case, we seem to be admitting that the age of religion as great social institution, community creed and world view, set of practices and values — all *that* is over and done with. We now live in a do-it-yourself age in which people have to evolve their own personal spirituality, and must no longer expect a great visible institution to do their thinking for them.

All this is disconcerting, but there are powerful considerations that point to such a conclusion. During the Enlightenment we became irreversibly committed to the relatively-new critical style of thinking, and to the related (but not identical) idea of freedom of thought. These ideas abolish any notion of loyally believing what everyone says, what Tradition tells us, or what Authority commands us to believe. One moves instead into a new territory where, on every issue whatever, there is a balance of probabilities, a spectrum of possible views (even the most implausible of which seems always to be held by *somebody*), and a gradually shifting consensus — but no certainty. As Lessing and Kierkegaard saw clearly enough, this puts an end to the appeal to historical evidence in support of dogmatic belief. In the long run, as I have already admitted, it is clear that the whole truth of Christianity cannot continue to be made to rest upon the truth of certain historical statements about Jesus of Nazareth in the way it has been said to do in the past.

I have allowed for this by saying that in future we should see religious beliefs not as metaphysical or historical truths, but simply as maxims of life and guiding pictures that each person can and must adopt and check out for herself. Critical faith requires that you must become your own arbiter in matters of belief.

Along these lines, can we perhaps imagine how the religion of the future may be both critical and communal? Being critical, the faith of the future will not make any quasi-factual claims of the sort that open debate always erodes away. Instead it will consist only of a collection of maxims of life and guiding pictures which each person is free to adopt and check out individually. But we don't all have to learn exactly the same set of lessons in the same order: on the contrary, many different journeys can be made in different directions across the same landscape. We travellers start from different places, and may seem to be going in different directions; but in the end we may find ourselves converging. We've passed through many of the same places, in the course of our varied personal journeys. So it may be possible to imagine how there can be considerable variety, and entire personal freedom, within a shared tradition.

However, I must confess that I have abandoned a great deal that is still precious to many others. We have to give up supernatural doctrine, we have to give up historical claims about revelations and great events in the remote past, and we have to give up all ideas of a sovereign Authority that defines a Final Truth. There ain't no Final Truth.

樂 樂 樂 樂 樂

It seems reasonable to regard our emotions as rooted in our biology. Like other animals, we are touchy, nervous creatures, apt to see in almost any sudden event a potential threat to our well-being. We are very sensitive to the gains or pains that may accrue to us through the approach or withdrawal of a possible predator, or mate, or rival, or food, or place of shelter, or whatever. In short, our emotional life is coloured by constant, anxious self-concern.

It is, I suggest, language and culture that have had the effect of making us into bigger worriers than any other animal. They greatly amplify the turbulence of our emotional life by giving us more and more to worry about. We start to worry about **It All**, and our feeling-life goes cosmic. But when we start having feelings about our attitudes towards **It All**, or Everything, or **Life**, we begin to outsoar and break free from the self, and from things particular and empirical. That's a liberation.

Thus we can say, not only that religion is cosmic emotion, but also that religious feeling is feeling that in going cosmic has found ways of breaking free from anxious self-concern. Religious feeling is feeling that has become liberated, universal, blissful. One loves — but in an open and non-fixated way. One feels grateful, but not to any individual: one feels grateful *to* Life, *for* Life: one feels open and nonobjective gratitude. And so on: it is of course vital to my account that genuine religious feeling is 'non-realistic': it does not attempt to turn the religious object back into a being, a *person*. That would make religious love fixated, i.e. idolatrous. So I should say firmly and explicitly that there is not another person out there. As Spinoza puts it, he who loves God must not expect his love to be returned. Divine love is completely open and indiscriminate. Religious feeling does not involve detecting and responding to another person out there. Out there, there is only **It All**, infinite scattering.

We need examples, to show how raw biological emotion is converted into unselfed, nonobjective religious feeling, and I begin with a simple and vivid one — the conversion of our biological fear of heights and of falling into awe and wonder before the Sublime in nature.

Have you ever tried to persuade a young animal or a baby to venture off the opaque carpet and onto a clear polished-glass floor through which one can see down through empty space? It's very difficult. Indeed, adult animals and humans also find it virtually impossible to step out and walk across a clear glass floor. Young children and animals will normally not even ascend an open staircase that has treads but no risers. In general, they and we demand a solid opaque foreground before our feet, and we feel dizzy and slightly sick if there is only a great void in front of us. We feel the same vertigo — a 'sensation of whirling and loss of balance'[49] — when we stand on the edge of a cliff or a high-rise building and look forwards and downwards.

But do we feel equally sick on a mountain peak? Seemingly not. A long cultural tradition has taught us rather to see mountain tops as holy places where the gods dwell. Centuries of mountain climbing for pleasure make us experience a yearning, soaring exhilaration amid that vast silent space — and I think we can see in this case that culture has somehow managed to convert a reflex biological feeling of dread and repugnance into a great feeling of spiritual exaltation (literally, 'raising up aloft'), from which any personal anxiety has gone.

In this simple example we see how culture — or religion — has the art of being able to convert raw biological feeling, the fear of falling, fear of heights, into a major spiritual experience. But just how is the trick done? Here is another example. The human eye tends by its anatomy to focus upon a central spot to which it pays very close attention. This is most often a human body, or more specifically a face, the expression on a face, and the eyes. When we look at a scene or a painting, our eyes then track around, typically from face to face, working out who everyone is, where they are coming from, where they are going to, and what is going on. We look for cues and we work out narrative hypotheses. In fact, we see a painting by searching it like a detective at a crime scene. At the back of one's mind there is the usual self-concern: How do I fit into this set up? What's in it for me? Thus our vision is ordinarily focussed and self-concerned, with a strong narrative interest. The world is a stage, on which we are trying to work out what is going on, and on which we are looking to play our own part.

However, during the past 120 years or so, many artists have produced works that strongly resist being read in the traditional way. These new-style works do not encourage the eye to track around, looking for clues. Instead they aim to unfocus our attention, to draw the eye in and drown it, to 'decentre' the attention and the selfhood of the spectator. Such paintings include Claude Monet's last impressionist works, Barnett Newman's great scarlet rectangles, and many big 'nihilistic' super-realist works of recent years — including giant photographs made with large-plate cameras by a number of artists currently working in the American urban landscape.

The traditional Western ways of composing, and of looking at, a painting followed the eye's natural, biological inclination. Focus equals Freudian fixation. We scan the scene, working out possible scenarios with a view to deciding what's in it for us. And in the West, Christian art has remained firmly 'natural' in its preoccupation with the human face and figure. But in the new tradition something much more Buddhist has come to the West — an attempt to create pleasure by decentring, scattering, or drowning the subject. It comes in at about the same time as pleasure in sunbathing: pleasure in gazing into the glittering blue void of a cloudless summer sky, pleasure in becoming emptied-out and vacant. But my earlier mention of big super-realist paintings and large-plate photographs of American office-blocks and suburban housing reminds me to add that in these cases the artist may sometimes be wanting us to experience the 'emptiness' as meaninglessness and spiritual desolation. It is often not clear, and the viewer of the scene must decide in each particular case. Either way, the general point here is that the effect of emptiness and unselfing, whether blissful or desolate, is produced by the techniques of an artist who guides our perception. One might compare this with the ways in which, both in Christianity and in Buddhism, people used to be taught to cultivate a form of prayer or meditation in which you stayed fully awake and attentive, whilst also being unselfed and emptied out. Terms such as 'silent regard' and 'mindfulness' were used to describe it.

Here, as in the first example, culture starts from the restless, erotically enquiring, potentially fixating male gaze, and finds ways of converting it into the resting, unselfed, cool, and religious kind of attentiveness.

Another example is secular, but of great contemporary importance. We are animals, and especially in springtime we are aware of what we variously describe as *libido*, 'rising sap', and the **feeling of being alive** (or in Wordsworth's phrase, 'the pleasure that there is in life itself': Chaucer might have called it 'lechery'). Now, the effect of a decent scientific education ought to be to expand and sublimate this very basic animal love of life into a passionate and thoroughly informed concern for our whole natural environment. As, indeed, we all know very well — which makes the vitally important point that the cultural/religious job of turning our biology into spirit needs to be done (and nowadays very often *is* being done) by science teachers.

In short, we can now see that much of culture is about equipping people for life in a state society by teaching them how to sublimate raw biological impulses into socially-preferable cool and universal dispositions —for example, when we reason people into converting the impulse to seek sudden and violent revenge into the cool passion for universal justice; or when we learn to sublimate anxiety into vigilance in caring for and maintaining social institutions of every kind. A less obvious, but very important, example is the way the establishment of great public museums and art galleries with free or cheap access has helped us habitually to separate aesthetic enjoyment from any taint of personal covetousness.

A conclusion needs to be drawn for education generally. By setting out to describe the religious concern in post-metaphysical and purely this-worldly terms, I have brought religion very close to culture. And, conversely, I have brought culture very close to religion. It was not by some sort of accident that in premodern times religion was the basis of high civilization: *it still is*. For when we study science, or art, or the law, or public administration, with a proper regard for what this training should mean both to us personally and to society, we are learning religious values; whereas, conversely, when we study the rather decadent (and of course entirely optional) subjects described as 'religions' in the modern syllabus, we will probably encounter little of any great religious significance. And this shrunken and sectarian conception of religion with which we seem to be cursed nowadays is damaging to the wider culture, which is apt to become unaware of the religious values on which it is still built.

I insist that these values — public space, public life, public service, public interest, common good, impartiality, and so on — are religious. They need a spirituality (in fact a non-realist religious practice) to maintain them, and always will.

Notes

1 See Georges Bataille, *Theory of Religion* (New York: Zone Books, 1992).

2 *The New Religion of Life in Everyday Speech* (London: SCM Press, 1999).

3 *The Meaning of It All in Everyday Speech* (London: SCM Press, 1999); *Kingdom Come in Everyday Speech* (London: SCM Press, 2000); *Life, Life* (Santa Rosa CA: the Polebridge Press, 2003).

4 'Traditionalism' is technically the doctrine (actually put forward by some Roman Catholic extremists in the early nineteenth century) to the effect that 'all metaphysical, moral and religious knowledge is based on a primitive revelation of God to man handed down in an unbroken tradition' (F.L. Cross (ed.), D.C.C., s.v.). Human reason has no power in itself to attain to any important truth: we are wholly dependent on Tradition.

5 As Professor D.E. Nineham has been saying in Britain for many years.

6 See Albert Schweitzer, *The Quest of the Historical Jesus*, First Complete Edition, ed. John Bowden (London: SCM Press, 2000).

7 For the Jesus-Seminar case against Schweitzer's theory, see for example Robert J. Miller (ed.) *The Apocalyptic Jesus: A Debate* (Santa Rosa CA: the Polebridge Press, 2001). For *The Dhammapada*, see the Penguin Classics edition (trans. Juan Mascaro, 1973), and compare it with the Polebridge Press's *Q-Thomas Reader* (ed. John S. Kloppenberg and others, 1990).

8 Published by the OUP.

9 See my *The Religion of Being* (London: SCM Press, 1998), c.4

10 I have lifted these two instructive quotations from J.M. Cohen and M.J. Cohen (ed.), *The Penguin Dictionary of Modern Quotations*, Second edition, 1980.

11 'Easy, going', with a comma between the two words, has been one of my favourite catchphrases for at least a decade. But it is, somehow, invariably misunderstood. I am using 'easy' in an American sense: one who is **easy, going** is untroubled about the fact that he is passing away, and knows it.

12 F.A. Lea, *The Tragic Philosopher: A Study of Friedrich Nietzsche* (New York, 1957; London, 1973); Alistair Kee, *Nietzsche Against the Crucified* (London: SCM Press, 1999).

13 In the closing pages of *Thus Spoke Zarathustra*, First Part.

14 For example, in *Jesus: A Revolutionary Biography* (San Francisco: Harper San Francisco, 1994).

15 Gilles Deleuze and Felix Guattari, *Anti-Oedipus* (London: Athlone Press, 1984).

16 Emil L. Fackenheim, *The Religious Dimension in Hegel's Thought* (Chicago and London: The University of Chicago Press, 1982 edition): a splendid and precious book.

17 *Life, Life* (Santa Rosa CA: the Polebridge Press, 2003), pp.43-46 and 147.

18 I use 'own' in this context to mean both possess, and confess, *and* assume moral responsibility for.

19 In his *Introduction* to my *Reforming Christianity* (Santa Rosa CA: the Polebridge Press, 2001), p.xii.

20 *The Varieties of Religious Experience* (London and New York: Longmans 1902), Lecture II (early editions, pp.27f.).

21 Matt 5:45.

22 *The Essence of Christianity* (1841; Eng. trans. by George Eliot, 1854).

23 *Theodicée* (1714).

24 I commend the Penguin Classics translation by A.J. Krailsheimer, first published in 1966 and still in print. See especially the first forty pages or so.

25 All this is splendidly and classically explained in Bronislaw Malinowski's essay 'Magic, Science and Religion', which first appeared in Joseph Needham (ed.) *Science, Religion and Reality* (1925), and has often been reprinted.

26 A good one-volume sketch of the vast cultural change here being referred to is still Edward Craig, *The Mind of God and the Works of Man* (Cambridge: the Cambridge University Press 1987).

27 Michel Foucault, *The Care of the Self: The History of Sexuality*, Volume Three (New York: Pantheon/Random House 1986; London: Allen Lane, the Penguin Press 1988).

28 For the ideas about ordinary language in the previous paragraph, see the later philosophy of Wittgenstein. For the material in this paragraph, see my *The New Religion of Life in Everyday Speech* (London: SCM Press 1999), and *Life, Life* (Santa Rosa CA: the Polebridge Press, 2003), especially the list of life-idioms in the Appendix.

29 See the double negation in the last two sentences of the four-book main text of *The World as Will and Representation* (1819, second edition 1844, third 1859).

30 See my *Reforming Christianity* (Santa Rosa CA: the Polebridge Press, 2001), pp.81-82.

31 In the language of that time, the battle between the Ancients and the Moderns was won decisively by the Moderns.

32 In *A Grammar of Assent* (1870).

33 Martin Amis, *The War against Cliché* (London: Jonathan Cape 2001; New York: Random House/Vintage 2002).

34 *Farewell.* The stanza continues:

Let no night
Seal thy sense in deathly slumber
Till to delight
Thou hast paid thy utmost blessing;

Since that all things thou wouldst praise
Beauty took from those who loved them
In other days.

Which (beneath all the poetic diction) is very close to certain themes in my
own writing. We are able to see our land as beautiful and to love it because we see
it with eyes that are influenced by a long line of naturalists, painters, and others
who have preceded us. Science in particular has hugely enriched and beautified
the world for us, by differentiating, describing, and theorizing it so minutely.

35 I name three of the species of butterfly that in England overwinter in the
adult form, usually emerging on the first sunny days in March.

36 See p.76, above.

37 Citations from T.F. Torrance (ed.) *The School of Faith: the Catechisms of the
Reformed Church* (London: James Clarke 1959), pp.5, 185.

38 *Paradiso*, XXXIII, 142-5.

39 See the opening pages of the *Nicomachean Ethics*.

40 Matt 5:8; *1 Cor* 13:12.

41 E.g., *Leviathan*, Part 1, cc.6, 7.

42 See my *Solar Ethics* (London: SCM Press 1995).

43 *Rules for the Direction of the Mind* (1628; not published in Descartes' lifetime); *Discourse on Method* (1637); *Meditations on First Philosophy* (1641).

44 *Leviathan* (1651) c.32.

45 'Mindhold', a coinage on the analogy of 'foothold', is a word I first learnt
from Elizabeth Anscombe.

46 When Nietzsche says this sort of thing he is referring to the developed
Latin Christian system of doctrine, which he hates, and which eventually under-
mines itself when we turn against it the morbid self-questioning and self-mistrust
that it taught us. Nietzsche also sometimes uses the word 'Christianity' for the
rather simple and direct, undogmatic and unmediated, way to happiness that was
taught by the original Jesus. For that, he feels a certain admiration, as do I.

47 Cited from 'the Oxford Wordsworth' — *Wordsworth: Poetical Works*, edd.
Thomas Hutchinson, revised by Ernest de Selincourt (Oxford: Oxford University
Press, 1936 and very often reprinted), p.734, col.2.

48 *Ibid.*, p.70, col.2, ll.33f.

49 From the definition in the *New Oxford Dictionary of English* (1998). The
word 'vertigo' is most commonly heard now mispronounced, and as the name of a
medical condition. The refusal of babies to crawl over a seeming 'visual cliff' was
first noted by Eleanor J. Gibson and Richard D. Walk in an article in *Scientific
American*, April 1960 (Vol. 202: 64-71). You can stand on a glass floor above a
great deal of empty space at the top of the communications tower in Toronto. It is
very queasy-making.

A Note about Books

Dictionaries

I begin with a note about dictionaries, because my 'democratic' approach to religious thought requires me to pay much attention to the way things are going in popular speech, and the student of idioms and stock phrases needs criteria by which to judge how well-established in the language a particular phrase is. We cannot rely only on a personal sense of familiarity; we need also to see a phrase, or topic, or question pursued in the media, and cited in dictionaries.

I use the well-known Oxford dictionaries, including *The Oxford English Dictionary*, Second Edition of 1989, reprinted with corrections, 1991; *The New Oxford Dictionary of English*, ed. Judy Pearsall, 1998; *The Oxford Dictionary of English Idioms*, ed. A.P. Cowie, R. Mackin and I.R. McCaig, 1993; and *The Oxford Concise Dictionary of Proverbs*, edited by John Simpson, 1982, reissued 1996. In addition to the well-known *Oxford Dictionary of Quotations*, I use *The Penguin Dictionary of Modern Quotations*, ed. J.M. and M.J. Cohen, Second Edition, New York: Penguin Books, 1980.

Very good evidence of the currency of phrases is the fact that foreigners need to learn them when they are being taught spoken English. TEFL books (Teaching English as a Foreign Language) are very useful, and the big Collins two-language popular dictionaries, English-French/French-English and English-German/German-English, have particularly full lists of phrases.

The outstanding work on slang is *The Cassell Dictionary of Slang*, ed. Jonathon Green, London: Cassell, 1998. Finally, the student must not forget that nowadays many good new phrases first enter the language as book, film and song titles. Again there are many standard reference works, and I favour *Halliwell's Film and Video Guide*, a new edition of which still comes each year from Harper Collins of London and New York. This class of phrases has the great advantage of coming each with a date attached. At least one is entitled to conclude that the phrase was already current at the time, or became current from the time, that the title was issued or published. So dated titles give a little help with the often-difficult question of dating generally.

In general, I must insist that the 'ordinary language' or 'democratic' theology and philosophy that I am trying to write cannot succeed unless we are as rigorous as the best journalists with our criteria for identifying topics and phrases, dating them, and establishing their currency.

Other Modern Works Referred To

Amis, Martin. *The War Against Cliché*. London: Jonathan Cape, 2001; New York: Random House/Vintage, 2002.

Bataille, Georges. *Theory of Religion*. New York: Zone Books, 1992.

Cohen, J. M. and M. J. (eds.) *The Penguin Dictionary of Modern Quotations*. Second Edition. London and New York: Penguin Books, 1980.

Brightman, F. E. (ed.) *The Preces Privatae of Lancelot Andrewes*. London: Longmans, 1903.

Craig, Edward. *The Mind of God and the Works of Man*. Cambridge, England and New York: Cambridge University Press, 1987.

Cross, F. L. (ed.) *The Oxford Dictionary of the Christian Church*. Oxford: Oxford University Press, 1957.

Crossan, John Dominic, *Jesus: A Revolutionary Biography*. San Francisco: Harper, 1994.

Cupitt, Don. *Solar Ethics*. London: SCM Press, 1995.

The Religion of Being. London: SCM Press, 1998.

The New Religion of Life in Everyday Speech. London: SCM Press, 1999.

The Meaning of It All in Everyday Speech. London: SCM Press, 1999.

Kingdom Come in Everyday Speech. London: SCM Press, 2000.

Reforming Christianity. Santa Rosa, CA: Polebridge Press, 2001.

Life, Life. Santa Rosa, CA: Polebridge Press, 2003.

Deleuze, Gilles and Guattari, Felix. *Anti-Oedipus*. London: Athlone Press, 1984.

Fackenheim, Emil L. *The Religious Dimension of Hegel's Thought*. Chicago and London: University of Chicago Press, 1982 edition.

Feuerbach, Ludwig. *The Essence of Christianity*, 1841; trans. George Eliot, London, 1854.

Foucault, Michel. *The Care of the Self: The History of Sexuality*, Volume Three. New York: Pantheon/Random House, 1986 and London: Allen Lane, the Penguin Press, 1988.

Gibson, Eleanor J. and Walk, Richard D. Article in *Scientific American*, April 1960, Vol. 202, pp.64-71.

Hutchinson, Thomas (ed.) *Wordsworth: Poetical Works*, revised by Ernest de Selincourt. Oxford: Oxford University Press, 1936 and very often reprinted.

James, William. *The Varieties of Religious Experience: A Study in Human Nature*. London and New York: Longmans, 1902 and many reprints.

Kee, Alistair. *Nietzsche Against the Crucified*. London: SCM Press, 1996.

Kloppenberg, John S. and Others. *Q-Thomas Reader*. Santa Rosa,. CA: Polebridge Press, 1990.

Krailsheimer, A. J. (ed. and tr.) *Pascal: Pensées*. London and New York: Penguin Books, 1966 and very often reprinted.

Lea, F. A. *The Tragic Philosopher: A Study of Friedrich Nietzsche*. New York, 1957; London, 1973.

Malinowski, Bronislaw. 'Magic, Science and Religion'; in Joseph Needham (ed.), *Science, Religion and Reality*, 1956, and then often subsequently reprinted in other collections.

Mascaro, Juan (ed. and tr.) *The Dhammapada*. Penguin Classics edn. London and New York, 1973.

Miller, Robert J. (ed.) *The Apocalyptic Jesus: A Debate*. Santa Rosa, CA: Polebridge Press, 2001.

Newman, J. H. *A Grammar of Assent*. 1870.

Opie, Iona and Peter. *The Love and Language of Schoolchildren*. Oxford: the Oxford University Press, 1959.

Schopenhauer, Arthur. *The World as Will and Representation*. 1819; second edition, 1844; third edition, 1859. Trans. E. F. J. Payne in Two Volumes, New York: Dover Publications, 1966 and regularly reprinted.

Schleiermacher, F. D. E. *On Religion: Speeches to its Cultured Despisers*. 1799, Eng. Trans. London, 1893; and as 'Addresses in Response to its Educated Critics', London, 1969.

Schweitzer, Albert. *The Quest of the Historical Jesus*, First Complete Edition, ed. John Bowden. London: SCM Press, 2000.

Torrance, T. F. (ed.) *The School of Faith: The Catechisms of the Reformed Church*. London: James Clarke, 1959.

Wittgenstein, Ludwig. *Tractatus Logico-Philosophicus*. Trans. By D.F. Pears and B.F. McGuinness. London: Routledge and Kegan Paul, 1974.

Index

Amis, M., 58
Andrewes, Lancelot, vii, 11f.
Aristotle, viii, 64
Angustine, 54
Austen, Jane, 8

Bataille, Georges, vii, 1
Belief, believe, 3f., 17ff.
Brightman, F. E., 12
Browning, E. B., 49
Buddha, 7f., 25, 69, 76

Calvin, J., viii
Chaucer, G., 77
Copernicus, N., 31
Coram, Thomas, 55
Crossan, J. D., 24

Dante Alighieri, viii, 64
Death, see Life and Death
Deleuze, G., 28
Democratic philosophy, viii, 32, 58
Descartes, Rene, 66f.
Dewey, Arthur, 36
Dewey, John, 15

Emotion, 37ff., 40f., 43, 54ff.
Emotional intelligence, viii, 56

Feuerbach, L., viii, 42, 51
Fleming-Williams, Ian, 29
Foucault, M., 50
Freud, S., 38

Galileo Galilei, 31, 66f.
God, 1, 3, 8f., 13, 18
Guattari, F., 28

Happiness, v, 12
 – eternal, vii, 12
Hegel, G. W. F., 21, 28, 50f., 71
Heidegger, M., 4, 15, 35
Hobbes, T., viii, 66ff.
Hume, David, 55
Holtzmann, 7

James, William, 40
Jesus Seminar, 7

Kant, I., 43, 50f., 71
Kazantzakis, N., 8
Kee, Alistair, 23
Kierkegaard, S., 73
Kingdom-era, 26f.

Lacan, J., 38
Lawrence, D. H., 3, 29, 38
Lea, F. A., 23
Leibniz, G. W., viii, 42
Lessing, G., 73
Life, see The Religious Object
 – and death, 31–36, 42–46
Luther, M. and K., 23, 31, 68

de la Mare, W., 61
Marx, K., 50f.
Monet, Claude, 60, 76
Mullan, Peter, 25

Newman, Barnett, 76
Newman, J. H., 56
Newton, Isaac, 54
Nietzsche, F., vii, 3, 8, 23f., 27, 29, 68

Obscenities, 10

Opie, Iona and Peter, 13f., 72
Ordinariness, 2, 13ff., 32, 52, 72

Pascal, B., 43
Plato, 46, 54, 71
Prayer, 12
Profanities, 8–11

Reason, rationality, 49, 56f.
– supernaturalism of reason, 43, 54, 57
– objective reason, 58, 71
Religion, theories of, vii, 1, 5
– as cosmic emotion, vii, 8ff., 40f.
– as joy in life, viii, 22f., 24, 31, 42
The Religious Object
– God, 3, 9, 13, 15
– Life, 3, 9, 15, 17
– It, It All, vii, 3, 12, 15
– Things, Everything, 15
– Existence, Being, 15
– Fate, luck, chance, fortune, hap, etc.,
    vii, 16
Religious Enquiry, new method of, 3ff.,
    31-33

Rousseau, J. J., 55
Sacred and profane love, vii, 10f., 27ff., 40
Schopenhauer, A., 37f., 53
Schweitzer, A., 7
Shaftesbury, A. A.Cooper, First Earl of,
    viii, 54
Shakespeare, W., 7
Solar ethics, living, solarity, viii, 31, 45,
    53f., 62
Spinoza, B. de, 75

Teleology, final causes, 63-66

Van Gogh, V., 40
Vertigo and the Sublime, 75
Virgo, John, viii, 59, 63

Weiss, J., 7
Wittgenstein, L., 2, 13, 15, 44
– on ordinary language, 2
Wordsworth, William, v, 71ff., 77
World love, viii, 42
Worship and speech acts, 12